STRAIGHT FROM GOD'S CORNER

By Brian L. Steenhoek

xulon
PRESS

Straight From God's Corner
by Brian L. Steenhoek

Printed in the United States of America

ISBN 978-1-60791-540-9

Unless otherwise indicated, scriptures references are taken from the NIV translation of the Bible. Copyright © 1996, published by Zondervan, and the KJV translation of the Bible. Copyright © 1995, published by Zondervan.

www.xulonpress.com

Butch and Kathy

May the Lord Use This
To Bless You and
Encourage You in Your
Walks.

In Christ,

Brian

Introduction

&p

Nine years ago, the Lord laid it upon my heart to start writing *Straight from God's Corner*, and out of obedience, I introduced my writing for the first time to close family and friends through email. It started with five readers, and has grown by God's grace to over 700 recipients to date, and is still growing. The Lord has now directed me to write this book you are about to read. It is compiled of several short true stories related to my life and walk with Jesus Christ. It is my heart's desire that the gift the Lord has given to me would encourage other Christians in their walk, and bring others to the saving knowledge of Him.

For 18 years, I chased after the American dream, to become wealthy, powerful, and leave a legacy in the world. In childhood, I knew the Bible stories from Sunday school and attended church, but never really had a personal relationship with Jesus Christ. I would like to share with you my personal testimony on how I became a Christian, so you will begin to understand who I am in Christ and experience the heart behind the writing in these stories.

I had this huge hole in my heart and tried to fill it with everything: sex, drugs, alcohol, and money. My ambition in life was to become a millionaire, have the most beautiful girl by my side, and experience life to the fullest. I was willing to do whatever it took, including stepping on anyone's back to attain my dream. The saying, "Looking out for number one," summed up my life in a nutshell. "Get rich overnight" was embedded in my thinking. I have tried it all. Nothing ever seemed to work, and the hole in my heart remained wide open.

Alcohol became a numbing agent, a form of escape when things were not going my way. One drink led to another, and soon I found myself comfortably numb to the things around me. I began to find my confidence in the drug and used it to take the edge off when needed. Drugs and alcohol were a powerful ego booster for me, and another avenue of release. Soon, I found myself addicted to the feeling of being high from the powerful combination of the two. But no matter how much I put in, nothing could fill the emptiness in my heart.

The lure of women became a sport to me, and I was always looking for the bigger prize, a trophy to show to my friends and family. Three nights a week and weekends were scheduled for hunting for the perfect catch. Money burned a hole in my pocket as I tried to keep up with the image I wanted to portray. I found myself buying things to impress people, to set me above everyone else. I would buy rounds of drinks (with only pennies in my pocket), thanks to a thing called credit. But no matter how much I spent, falling deeper into debt, no amount of money could satisfy the emptiness I felt.

I finally found the girl of my dreams, and after job-hopping several times, I was making exceptional money in a career, and I thought I had everything life could offer. I started another company with friends and just knew this would be our ticket to financial freedom. My girlfriend was a model and applying for the Miss Arizona pageant. We moved in together. We both had expensive tastes. I had to have the penthouse apartment, nice cars, designer clothes, and everything to maintain the image we wanted the world to see. The partying intensified, the debt increased, and there was still something missing.

Five years later, the Lord began to grab my attention. I lost my job due to the after-effects of partying, my fiancé left, the business failed, I filed bankruptcy, and almost lost everything. I was very angry and bitter, and my only comfort was in drugs and alcohol. My drinking increased, and I became more and more numb. My life had begun to spiral out of control. I was working odd jobs during the day, and partying at night with new friends. I would find myself waking up in someone else's house, on people's front lawns, or in my own car. The hole in my heart was still there. It only grew bigger, and the emptiness grew stronger.

One night, after passing out from drinking, I awoke at 3 o'clock in the morning, hearing something telling me, "Brian, if you continue down the path you are on, it will only lead to your death." I got up, still hung over, and looked into the mirror, only to discover death staring me in the face. I fell to my knees and began to weep, saying, "There has to be more to life than this!" Immediately, the thought of going to church surfaced in my mind. Maybe there would be an answer to my problems there. I grabbed the phone book and frantically scanned the pages. Corona Baptist Church jumped off the page at me. The church was one mile from my house, and something inside of my heart was driving me there.

Dressed in jeans, sandals, a concert shirt, and still hung over from the night before, I approached the church, but with hesitation, doubt, and fear. Thinking this was a crazy idea, I was ready to turn tail and run, when I heard a voice cry out to me, "Welcome to Corona Baptist Church." The pastor was running out to greet me with loving open arms, and invited me into his church. He introduced me to the singles group and invited me to stay for Sunday school and the service. The messages spoke volumes to me and opened my eyes to a new light. It seemed like they were designed just for me and my situation. I felt something different in my heart, and knew I needed to hear more.

I returned for the evening service early, and asked the pastor for a moment of time. We stepped into his office and sat down across from each other.

He asked me a simple question: "Brian, who is in control of your life?"

He grabbed a piece of paper and pen and drew a simple diagram reflecting the question. I released everything, all my anger, bitterness, and fear. I told him everything about my life and questioned the empty feeling I had been experiencing. He placed his hand on my shoulder, shared the Gospel, and introduced me to a man called Jesus Christ. I began to sob uncontrollably after hearing what this man did for me, and prayed a simple prayer, accepting him into my life. Almost instantly, the empty feeling in my heart disappeared and a new joy came over me like a flood. All my burdens were lifted, my sins were forgiven, and I was a new creation in Christ.

The power of the Holy Spirit living in my heart changed my life. In the first week of being a Christian, I stopped all addictive behaviors, ended relationships, and took a vow of purity with True Love Waits. My friends thought I lost my mind when I took several large trash bags and removed everything ungodly from my house. I eventually lost all my party friends, and had to face some lonely times. The Lord was good and introduced me to new Christian friends, who were instrumental in helping me walk daily with the Lord. I had finally found what I was looking for to fill the void in my life.

Twelve years ago, I accepted Jesus Christ into my life, and things have never been the same. He has instilled in me the gift of writing and speaking, and has called me to encourage, lift up, and share the words the Holy Spirit gives me. My walk with the Lord has not been easy, and I do not understand everything that happens. Through my divorce, I have discovered my fear of confrontation, passivity, and lack of confidence. The Lord has changed me and called me to be a warrior for Him, roaring for His Kingdom. He has given me the tools to help wake hearts and restore brokenness. God has allowed me to use the experiences in my life, tie them to His Word, and encourage anyone who reads or hears them. I just want to be obedient to the calling of the Lord on my life and hear the words from Him face-to-face, "My good and faithful servant."

I give God all the glory, and thank Him for using me in a simple way. I thank my parents, Dick and Judy Steenhoek, who have always been there for me and have loved me unconditionally; my wonderful brother, Mark Steenhoek, who has always been an inspiration to me. I am thankful for friends and family who have encouraged me to continue my writing over the years. Thanks to all the recipients of *Straight from God's Corner,* and their encouraging replies to my email messages. Thanks to Xulon Publishing, who helps make dreams come true. Finally, a sincere thank you to all the readers:

may this book encourage you, lift you, and introduce or deepen your walk with a man named Jesus Christ.

Fighting for God,

Brian L. Steenhoek

Table of Contents

Comments from Readers of Straight From God's Corner:

How *Straight from God's Corner* has impacted my life: When I first saw your name, it was on a Christian mingle site. I thought I wanted to meet an individual for a relationship, when what I really needed was to do that with God. Soon after receiving a few of your God letters, which I love, I was diagnosed with metastatic ocular melanoma (at that time 4 tumors to the liver, but now 8). Due to those very letters and the powerful lesson/prayer you sent, I am more ok now with 8 liver melanoma tumors than I was when I met you. That is because of the way you write. You led me to a deeper relationship with God. You relate real life to religion in a way that I feel like I am there. It is that powerful for me. I am forever grateful to your writings and had better receive a signed copy!! May you be blessed in your writings and your book, just as I have been, to fill the void by loving God.
Sincerely, L.M.

My life has been really impacted by your site. I feel God uses your devotions to speak to me daily and clearly. And I love sharing them w/people in my life. I print, copy, paste, and forward them on a regular basis. Praise God for having such a faithful servant in you.
G.C.

How very blessed you are! Continue your fight and stay the course. Glad to see God continues to do great things with your talent. "During

uncertainty, when God is patiently awaiting my voice, your words of encouragement have prompted me to thank him for the battles!"
Peace to you always, Brian! L.W.

So many times the Holy Spirit has used your writing to bring me back to a place of peace in my life. The battle that wages in my mind, filled with the lies of defeat from the enemy, threatens my sanity at times. Just as with everything the Lord does, He sends a message right on time. This reminder to put on the whole armor of God is just what I needed today. To be reminded of my part in receiving my defense against unwanted attacks.
Thanks and God bless! V.S.

I have been blessed with the insight and wisdom the Lord has given to Brian as he ties his personal experiences to the Word of God. Each "corner" is filled with nuggets of gold and drips with anointing as sweet as honey.
T.D.

I have found your stories, parables inspirational! As a spiritual person they seem to apply to daily modern every day situations. Thank you for sharing these with me, I have found them very
in spiritual! Inspiring!
Blessings, J.S.G.

Brian's call to be a "Warrior for Christ" has surely inspired many of us in our daily walk in faith, or in search of God. And his faith-fulness and willingness in being God's vessel in writing *Straight from God's Corner*, has shown not only his own character, but also through his own experiences we get a glimpse of our own heart... to stand in a place where we can embrace our own character, while escaping the grasp of a world that wants nothing more than to devour us and to keep us weak.
M.W.

Brian has the ability to look at everyday life through the lens of Scripture and see God's hand at work. Whether experiences from

childhood or from adulthood, Brian's perspective always makes me stop and worship God for His wonderful grace and working in my life!
R.S.

Brian, I am REALLY excited about your book coming out! I look forward to reading what you have on your heart every month. I get other scripture messages from Crosswalk and other places off the Internet, and read them before I begin work every morning, but yours is always more personal and brings God's word to me in a way that I can apply to my life on a daily basis. With your book coming out, does that mean we will no longer get your emails? I really hope they don't stop - they are such a source of strength for me. Thank you so very much for being there for me so many times when I needed to hear from God in just the way you could say it.
M.N.

Your letters are so very humbling because you are so out front about your life. Your great testimonies will continue to bless those that are making breakthroughs in their own lives. You remind me of the psalmist David, and as you know, not a very large man in stature, but he conquered greatly against his enemies. You go, David, get those Goliaths!
May the Lord Bless the words of your work.
West Coast Reader,
V.R.

"No More Running"

Isaiah 54:17

"No weapon that is formed against thee shall prosper; and every tongue that shall rise against thee in judgment thou shalt condemn."
- KJV

S ick feeling in my stomach, fear beginning to set in, I made my way to the bus. I quickly got on and took the closest seat to the door, trying to stay near the aisle. The bus would quickly fill up and I knew he was coming. He was the bully who always picked on me, stole my lunch money, or just picked on me for no apparent reason. I can still recall the day I was minding my own business when I heard him state from the seat behind me, "I am going to beat you up as soon as you step off this bus, Brian." Immediately, I felt even more sick to my stomach and was planning in my mind how to escape my imminent death.

I was a freshman in high school who looked like I was still in grade school. I weighed 120 lbs., soaking wet, was 5' 3", and could fit in a school locker. I was involved in the ROTC program and they had to make a custom uniform for me. I was called every name in the book and must have had a huge target painted on my back, as I tended to attract all the bullies. The only way to and from school was the bus, and almost every day I experienced some kind of adventure. Maybe that is why I can really relate to the movie, *Forest Gump*, when his friend shouted, "Run, Forest, run!"

The bus slowly made its way home and it seemed like it took hours. I could feel his eyes locked on me, and I was wondering what he was thinking. I did not dare look back, as I did not want to give him any more excuses for wanting to beat me up. I could hear him making comments to his friends, followed with an evil laugh. He had picked a day when I was in my ROTC uniform, so I had an immediate disadvantage. No tennis shoes only my almost-brand-new military shoes. How was I going to escape, what was I going to do now? The bus stop was several hundred yards from the comfort of home. The bus stopped and I immediately pushed my way to the front of the bus, exiting first, and never looked back. Some friends said I looked like a tornado ripping across the desert.

As Christians, we have a bully to deal with on a daily basis, and he does have a target painted on our backs. But the good news is that we do not have to run anymore. The devil has been trying to beat me up and discourage me from completing this book project. There have been many times over the years I have not written for months, as the enemy has had a strong foothold on my mind, convincing me I was not good enough. There was even a time when I completely lost all my email addresses for the people I send *Straight From God's Corner* to, and had to start over. The one thing I have noticed during those times was the Lord always brought me to a point of victory over the enemy, and I am excited to see my book in the final stages of being published.

So if we are feeling ill to our stomachs and have fear racing through our veins, we need to pull out the big weapons to defeat the bullies trying to come against us. Each morning, we need to put on the armor of God that the Lord has sitting out for us. He has given this to us to prevent the enemy from penetrating and getting a foothold on us physically, mentally, and spiritually. There are specific purposes for each piece, so we need to don all the armor. Let me encourage us to stop running and begin to stand up with the helmet of salvation, breastplate of righteousness, girdle of truth, sandals of peace, shield of faith, and the sword of the Spirit, drawn against the enemy, and continue to stand, knowing we have the victory in Jesus Christ.

Do not allow the enemy to steal our dreams and visions, or detour us from the Lord's ultimate plan for our lives. We are in a battle, and the enemy wants to destroy us and render us useless for the Kingdom. When the enemy gets a foothold in our lives, we are the ones who allowed it to happen by not being prepared. Let's get up every morning, put on the armor of God, and walk victoriously in his power. We can do all things through Jesus Christ who strengthens us.

Lord Jesus,

Thank You for being our strength and protector. Through one drop of Your blood, we were saved by Your grace, and there is nothing, not even man, who can snatch us from Your hands. You have given us the tools to use in battle, and it is my prayer we would take this battle seriously and take the precautions for our safety on a daily basis. I pray there would be no more running, only standing in Your power to defeat the enemy that will comes against us.

"Be Still"

Luke 10:38 – 42

"Now while they were on their way, it occurred that Jesus entered a certain village, and a woman named Martha received and welcomed Him into her house. She had a sister named Mary, who seated herself at the Lord's feet and was listening to His teaching. But Martha [overly occupied and too busy] was distracted with much serving; and she came up to Him and said, Lord is it nothing to You that my sister has left me to serve alone? Tell her then to help me [to lend a hand and do her part along with me]! But the Lord replied to her saying, Martha, Martha you are anxious and troubled about many things. There is need for only one or but a few things. Mary has chosen the good portion [that which is to her advantage], which shall not be taken away from her." – AMP

A Bavarian king would soon be arriving at the Hilton Hotel in Las Vegas. The whole room-service department was placed on high alert, and we were told to be at our very best when servicing this guest. The room-service captain assigned us to meet the demands of this king, and every request would be to his satisfaction. Hotel management put out a special memo to the entire staff, and the owner sacrificed his personal penthouse for this special guest's stay.

I received a room-service call ticket at midnight, and it was the King, wanting a barrage of items sent to his suite. There were so many, I needed assistance preparing the order. Panic set in, time was ticking away, and I did not want anything to go wrong with this order. I was literally running from one end of the kitchen to the other gathering items for the order. Five pounds of Alaskan King Crab legs, chilled caviar with a certain special bread, an array of specially cooked items, which had our cooks working in a frenzy, and several kinds of beverages and specialty drinks. The entire staff was in an uproar over this one order, like an out-of-control tornado.

We brought up three full carts of food to the suite. Three other staff members and I helped set up and serve the King. Upon arriving to the suite, the King's assistant gave us specific orders of how the King wanted the food to be presented and served. I was instructed to crack open five pounds of crab for him and place them on a bed of ice, and garnish with other shelled seafood. He wanted everything placed in a certain way and heated at a specific temperature. Needless to say, our whole staff was richly rewarded, but in my opinion, it was not worth the time.

As Christians, we get so caught up in preparing for the King, and forget the most important thing. We at times find ourselves trying to please the King for all the wrong reasons, and wind up running in a panic to meet what we feel the King has requested. I have found myself getting involved in a barrage of Christian-themed outreach activities, and tend to over-commit to the needs of the church. There have been many times I found myself in a panic to meet the different schedules. Missing an event leads to guilty feelings of not participating in furthering the Kingdom. We feel we will be richly rewarded for all of our efforts in furthering the Kingdom and that is true, but I personally find myself being drawn away from the most important thing.

For several weeks, I have been seeking wisdom and discernment from the Lord, and He has recently spoken to me through the above Scripture passage. Jesus is telling me to be still and sit at His feet and listen to what He has to say, to love Him first, and then allow His love to well up and flow through me, and finally further His Kingdom by showing others His love in me. He resides in our hearts, and He only desires one thing: To be in a close, loving, personal relationship with His creation. He does desire we further His Kingdom, but does not want us to compromise our personal time with Him. In reality, the Lord does not really need our help to accomplish anything, He can feed five thousand with a snap of his fingers, as He can do every-thing beyond anything we can think or imagine. He would rather we sit as His feet and seek Him with all our hearts, than to have us run in a million different directions, trying to please Him with our works.

If you are tired of trying to find out what the will of the Lord is for your life … listen closely. He desires for you and me to seek Him with all of our heart, mind, and soul. Jesus wants us to put Him first in our lives, over everything else that draws our attention away from Him. So if you are tired physically and mentally, like I was, stop, and "Be Still" at His feet, and listen to what He has to say to you. Jesus desires our love and needs nothing else. He instructed us to love Him first, and love our neighbors as we love ourselves second. By seeking the Kingdom in our hearts first, we will find everything else falling into place according to His will. Who knows what the blessings will be? Be assured that they will be well worth our time spent one-on-one with Him.

Lord Jesus,

Thank You for making everything so simple. Thank you for giving us wisdom and discernment through Your Word, and for showing me a simple way to find Your will for my life. I pray others would realize that Your will is for Your children to sit at Your feet and listen to Your voice, instead of running in a million different directions, assuming what pleases You, only to find that they are missing out on divine appointments with You. All You want is for us to come into Your presence and simply say, "I love you, Lord, and I do not need anything today."

"Beautiful Swan"

2 Corinthians 5:17

"Therefore if any person is [ingrafted] in Christ (the Messiah) he is a new creation (a new creation all together); the old [previous moral and spiritual condition] has passed away. Behold, the fresh and new has come!" – AMP

I am sure you are familiar with the fable of the ugly duckling. It is about a family of ducks, one being born black, and immediately standing out as the ugly duckling. The children of the family and the community shunned the little duckling. The duckling made every attempt to fit in with his brothers and sisters, but was not accepted. This little duckling had a very hard childhood and was convinced he would always stick out like a sore thumb. The mother duck, on the other hand, did not see her little duckling as different, and loved it just the same as the others. She knew this little duckling was very special and would one day prove it to the world.

There are several people I know, including myself, who at one time or another felt or now feel they were or are ugly ducklings. I can relate to having a very difficult time fitting in at school. I was the kid in high school who looked like a little boy, weighed 120 lbs., had braces, and was not confident with people. Can you relate to my story? I felt like an ugly duckling, and most people made fun of me or picked on me for spite. I must have been walking around with a target painted on my shirt, because I always attracted the bullies. I made every attempt to fit into society, joined clubs, and did things I really did not want to partake in. I was that kid who was picked for dodge ball last because I was the only one left to be picked.

I know several people can relate to this scrutiny growing up, or can relate to it now. I found myself running home to my mother's nest and finding comfort under her wing. She would assure me that I was very special and was destined for great things. I love the ending of the story: the little ugly duckling grows up to be the most beautiful swan for the entire world to see.

I, too, was transformed from ugly to beautiful, the moment I accepted Jesus Christ as my Savior. Jesus took away all my ugliness and replaced it with his splendor. The exciting news is that he is still working on me through his grace and mercy. I am a work in progress, and he would love to work in your life, too. He can take away all your ugliness and transform you into the beautiful swan you were created to be. He loves to work from the inside out and focuses on the heart.

There are many dimensions that must be developed for us to become extraordinary. We are all a work in progress, and God has great things destined for us. God delights in finding those who view themselves as insignificant, and raises them up to be mighty warriors for His Kingdom. If we continue thinking we are an ugly duckling, we will stay ugly. Our thoughts become our beliefs, and we act on our beliefs. If you believe you are nothing, then you will be nothing. Think like a beautiful swan, know that you are beautiful, inside and out. Swim gracefully, with the Lord by your side, with your head held high, and know that YOU were created for great things, according to His will!

Lord Jesus,

Thank You for accepting us the way we are, no matter what we have done. Thank you for Your blood that washes all the ugliness away and transforms us into beautiful swans. I pray that we remember who we are in You, Christ, and swim in Your grace with our heads held high.

"I Never Knew You"

Matthew 7:21

"Not every one that saith unto me. Lord, Lord, shall enter into the Kingdom of heaven; but he that doeth the will of my Father which is in heaven." – KJV

He sat polishing his sheriff's badge as my brother and I watched. The shine on his black cowboy boots was rich, dark, and you could almost see your reflection in them. His black Stetson hat was shaped perfectly, and the band around it was decorated with silver squares, shining like his polished badge. He took his black leather vest from the closet, carefully pinned his badge to the chest, and slipped his harmonica and pocket watch in the pockets. Finally, he secured his gun belt around his waist, tying the leather strap around his leg, holding the gun in place, and putting silver bullets in the empty loops on the back.

Annually, my Uncle Fred played the role of the sheriff on Western Day in his trailer park. My brother and I loved to participate and play along in his adventure. He would always tell us stories and keep our minds racing with exciting new things, each time we would visit. He could entertain us for hours, and boy, could he play a harmonica. Uncle Fred had a huge heart for the people in his trailer park, and knew everyone by name. He could even summarize what transpired in their lives. He would tip his cowboy hat to all the ladies and greet the men with a strong, firm handshake.

In his late eighties, he was diagnosed with Alzheimer's disease and progressively forgot things. There were several times when he would get things mixed up concerning the stories he had told us over and over before. One year, our Aunt Wilma had to show him how to put on his vest, hat, and gun for his favorite day, and eventually he could no longer play the role or remember Western Day. His harmonica remained in its box, coated with dust, never to be played again. During his last days, before going home to be with the Lord, he said to me one time, "I never knew you, who are you?" I looked deep into his eyes and replied, "It's me, Uncle Fred. Brian." Those eyes, once gleaming with adventure and full of life, were now empty and cold.

Nothing else seemed to matter to me, and all the years I had known Uncle Fred were now treasured memories. Even though I knew he was fighting this disease, to hear those words from him crushed me.

Could you imagine Jesus looking right into our eyes and saying, "I never knew you, depart from me, you that work iniquity"? But Lord, it's me. I attended church every Sunday, prayed, and did many great works. What must we do to prevent the loving eyes of Jesus turning from us on that day? We must do the will of our Father the Creator. What, we may be asking ourselves, what is the will of our Creator? It is very simple.

The Lord gave us the two greatest commands, which all other commandments hang from. We were created for one purpose: to love the Lord God with all our hearts, souls, and minds, and to love our neighbors as we love ourselves. It has nothing to do with going to church, reading the Bible, or doing good deeds, but has everything to do with love. Love produces good fruit. If we continue to read in Matthew, we will notice that doing things in love is like building a house on a strong rock, not to be shaken by any storm. Jesus desires that we just love on him and each other, so when Jesus looks deep into our eyes on that day, He will see His reflection staring back at Him.

Lord Jesus,

Thank You for making everything so simple to understand, and for demonstrating Your love for us through Your death and resurrection. I pray we would find the simple truth in Your Word, and see it is all about a loving, personal relationship with You and sharing Your love for us with others. It is my desire, in that day you talk about in Matthew, that all would know You personally, and none would be turned away after hearing those words: "I never knew you, depart from me."

"Prayer for Us"

Luke 24:46-47

"And said unto them, Thus it is written, and thus it behoved Christ to suffer, and to rise from the dead the third day: And that repentance and remission of sins should be preached in his name among all nations; beginning at Jerusalem." – KJV

John 17:1

"These words spake Jesus, and lifted up his eyes to heaven and said, Father, thy hour is come; glorify thy Son, that thy Son also may glorify thee: As thou hast given him power over all flesh, that he should give eternal life to as many as thou hast given him." – KJV

Stepping on my tiptoes, reaching for the toothpaste, grabbing my Superman toothbrush from the sink, I prepared to brush my teeth. My Snoopy pajama bottoms were pulled up around my waist and rolled at the bottom, as they were one size to big for me. I finished my hygiene routine, and was getting ready for sleep when my dog jumped up on the end of my bed, wagging his tail. Pulling down the clean covers, fluffing my pillow, I climbed into bed and pulled the covers back up to my neck.

My parents entered my room and asked, "Brian did you say your prayers?" I had totally forgotten, and jumped out of my bed to kneel down and pray. Both my parents got down on their knees to pray with me. Bowing my head, with closed eyes, I folded my hands in front of me and prayed, "Now I lay me down to sleep, I pray the Lord my soul to keep. If I die before I wake, I pray the Lord my soul to take." Then I prayed for my family and friends, my dog, and my other stuff. I prayed for everything that was near and dear to my heart.

Do you realize Jesus did that for us over 2,000 years ago? Getting down on His knees, lifting His eyes to heaven, He intervened for those most near and dear to His heart, and that petition was prayed for all of God's creation past, present, and future. Part of his prayer in John 17 says this: "Neither pray I for these alone, but for them also which shall believe on me through their word; That they all may be one; as thou, Father, art in me, and I in thee, that they also may be one in us; that the world may believe that thou has sent me"

Jesus was praying his last prayer for us before facing his death at Calvary, as recorded in the book of John. This prayer was so intense, and the burden so heavy, He asked his Father in heaven to remove the cup before Him three times, but gladly accepted his Father's will so we could be in fellowship with the Lord for eternity. Other books of the Bible describe the experience causing drops of blood to form on His brow. I can only image what stress would cause blood to drip from His forehead. You and I were on His mind and heart, as He did not want to see one of His Father's children lost to the devil.

Close your eyes and meditate on the Lord Jesus being on His knees, praying specifically for you and I so we could be with Him forever. Just know he had all of us individually by name on His mind, and we had not even been born yet. He was not lying in a comfortable bed with warm covers pulled to His neck, forgetting to pray. He was up before dusk with His disciples, who could not even stay awake. He got down on the dirty ground and sweated blood for us, then hours later bled and died for us, to give us the free gift of eternal life.

Lord Jesus,

Thank You for keeping all Your Father's creation on Your mind and centering everything You are on us. As we celebrate Easter and Your resurrection, let us be reminded what You went through to give us the free gift of eternal life that can be claimed by simply asking You to come into our lives and live in our hearts. Thank you for being obedient to Your Father's plan and not giving up on us. I still cannot imagine everything You went through for us. May we be reminded, each time we get down on our knees, of the prayer you prayed that early morning on our behalf.

"Being Dragged"

Ephesians 6:10

"In conclusion, be strong in the Lord [be empowered through your union with Him]; draw your strength from Him [that strength which His boundless might provides]." - AMP

சுழ

Floating in the water, hands gripped firmly on the handle, I prepared to ski. I felt the motor kick into gear, and simultaneously the rope become taut. Slowly being dragged behind the boat, I gave the thumbs up and waited for the launch. It had been years since I had water skied, and I was thinking, "How hard could it be….it's like riding a bike, you never forget."

Water gushing all around me, I attempted to get up the first time. I was being dragged behind the boat like a rag doll and had to release from the rope to prevent myself from drowning. Since I was unsuccessful in my attempts to get up on one ski, I had to eventually resort to starting on two skis before dropping one to slalom around the lake. With each attempt, I tried to access my body's position and tweak my technique to get out of the water, but I kept doing something wrong and couldn't quite figure it out.

After numerous attempts, I was able to get up and enjoy a ski around the lake. I just had to submit to the boat and allow the power of the engine to pull me out of the water. I recall an attempt when I tried to pull the boat to me, leading to a mouthful of water and almost losing my shorts. I had to position my body just right and apply the right amount of weight to the back of my ski. It felt very awkward at first, as I wobbled back and forth like a fishing lure being pulled through the water. But when the correct amount of power was applied from the engine, everything fell into place, and I popped right to the surface with little resistance.

Sometimes we try to pull the power towards us, instead of allowing the power to gravitate to us. Does this sound familiar? Have you been unsuccessful in getting out of the water? Maybe we have not positioned ourselves correctly and have been trying to get ourselves out of a situation, instead of allowing the engine, Jesus, to do the work for us. We have to position ourselves in God's Word and put all our weight on the Lord, then hang on and enjoy the ride.

Each time I try to do something under my own strength, I wind up with a mouthful of water and almost lose my shorts. Let me ask you a question: Whose power are you relying upon? Life can become frustrating at times, and we may think we can't get up. The good news is, in our weakness, God's strength will lift us up and sustain us. Do not worry about trying to get up. Focus on the engine that will. The task ahead of you is never as great as the power behind you.

Lord Jesus,

Thank You for being our strength and power. Forgive us for trying to do things in our own strength, only resulting in a mouthful of water. I pray we would stop trying to pull the boat, and allow the boat to pull us. I pray we would learn to position ourselves and allow You to do the work in and through us.

"My Best Friend"

John 15:13

"No one has greater love [no one has shown stronger affection] than to lay down (give up) his own life for his friends." - AMP

John 15:15

"I do not call you servants (slaves) any longer, for the servant does not know what his master is doing (working out). But I have called you My friends, because I have made known to you everything that I have heard from my Father. [I have revealed to you everything that I have learned from Him.]" - AMP

Rick and I were best friends throughout high school. Every day after school, we would experience a new electrifying adventure together. An exciting idea would surface between us, and we both were up for the challenge. We were young, wild and crazy, taking on the world one day at a time. Rick was a friend who was always there for me, even in the hard times. I could always count on his trust and loyalty.

I awoke this morning wondering what Rick may be up to these days. After graduation, leaving for the military, I lost track of my best friend. Now thinking about it, I have had several friends who have vanished over the years. Some were considered best friends for several years, but circumstances have separated us, and both parties have been too lazy to stay in touch. There have been a couple of instances of hearing through the grapevine an update on a friend who at one time was very close to me.

It is sad the way we go through life, making and losing friends, and most people we know have been business acquaintances. I can count on one hand the true friends I have in this world. There is only one friend who has never left me nor forsaken me, and His name is Jesus Christ. He is my best friend, and I can always count on Him being with me forever. He has never left my side, holds me close to his heart, and protects me with His right hand. He has been with me through the hard times, wiping tears from my eyes, and calming my fears.

I thought I knew what a best friend was, until I personally accepted Jesus Christ as my Savior. I have lost several friends in the course of my life and several were just using me to get what they wanted in life. The day I accepted Christ, I lost some of my closest friends, and quickly discovered they were not true friends after all. Jesus sees us as best friends, and He will be the greatest friend we will ever have. He will never disappear, lose interest, or be lazy about staying in contact with us. We can wake up each morning knowing He will always be walking by our side, taking on new, exciting adventures with us!

Lord Jesus,

Thank You for laying down Your life for us so we can call You our "Best Friend." Thank you for always being there for us, promising to never leave our side, and being the greatest best friend we could ever have. I pray we would reciprocate the friendship You bestow upon us, and we would be excited to get up each day and spend it with You.

"Blowing Bubbles"

Proverbs 18:20-21

"A man's [moral] self shall be filled with the fruit of his mouth; and with the consequence of his words he must be satisfied [whether good or evil]. Death and life are in the power of the tongue, and they who indulge in it shall eat the fruit of it [for death or life]." - AMP

The expressions on my parents' faces spoke a thousand words, not to mention what the guests were thinking as they looked on in disbelief. Everyone looked like a bunch of deer staring into an oncoming car's headlights. It seemed like time froze, and all eyes were locked on me. My mother turned beet red with embarrassment, and my father looked very disappointed. I was in hot water.

At a very young age, in anger, I screamed at the top of my lungs a curse *&^%$# word towards my brother. My excuse, "It just came out, Mom." Immediately, she grabbed me by my toothpick-sized arm and led me into the house. At first I thought Mom was going to deal with me, until a glance through the crowd showed my father excusing himself from the guests and following closely behind us.

"Where did you learn that word?" my father asked in a stern voice. No reply came from my lips as I gave my mom the sad face. Again he asked, "Where did you learn that word, Brian?"

I finally replied under pressure, "From a friend at school."

He explained to me how things we say can be positive or negative toward people, and bad words only get us in trouble. The word I said was bad, and I now would face the consequences for my actions. I received due punishment and learned a valuable lesson. Soap tasted terrible.

The words we speak can either lift people up or cut them down. Sometimes the things we say or do can impact lives in a negative way, and leave them scarred for life. God desires we speak loving words, not death-filled words toward one another. I wonder what the look is on God's face when we speak harsh words toward one another. His ears love to hear loving things come from our mouths, and He rejoices when we do things in love. His Word teaches us everything that comes from our lips will satisfy our bellies. What does this really mean? If we speak good, positive, loving things, then our soul will be full of love, but when we speak bad, negative, hateful things we will be full of hate.

If we speak love, we will produce love, and if we speak evil, we will produce evil and fall into sin. Let's not give the enemy ground. Capture every thought and word before it escapes your lips, and glorify God with the fruit that comes from within us. We need to ask the Holy Spirit for wisdom and discernment when facing a situation, and remember the words we speak will be planted in the hearts of the people you speak them to. We need to remember the words we speak will come to pass in our lives, so only allow positive words and actions to flow from us.

Lord Jesus,

Thank You for Your words being planted as seeds of love in our hearts. Thank You for loving us so much that You died for us on the cross. I pray we would live by Your example in your word and produce loving words from our lips to lift up each other. I pray we would protect our minds and hearts with Your armor, not allowing the enemy to gain any ground. Lord, be glorified by the fruit within us.

"Bound, Entangled, and Exhausted"

Hebrews 12:1

"Therefore then, since we are surrounded by so great a cloud of witnesses [who have borne testimony to the Truth], let us strip off and throw aside every encumbrance (unnecessary weight) and that sin which so readily (deftly and cleverly) clings to and entangles us, and let us run with patient endurance and steady and active persistence the appointed course of the race that is set before us." – AMP

Taking undersized strides, combating rough terrain, the prisoner made his getaway. The chains shackled between his feet and wrists were silenced, clutched in his sweaty grip, as he scurried to the closest hiding place he could find. Sodden with perspiration, eyes ablaze from the sweat and dirt, he managed to find a deserted shack in the thick of the woods. Exhausted and fatigued, he stooped down to catch his breath, and relieve the pain in his lower back. The weight of the chains had become overbearing as the shackles dug into his flesh. He needed a breather, but knew the posse would soon be hunting for him.

Anxiously, he searched for anything to help him break loose from the bonds of prison. After several desperate, unsuccessful attempts with different inert objects, he quickly became physically and mentally exhausted. With raw, blistered hands, he cleared a place to rest and regain his strength. Closing his eyes for a moment, he was immediately awakened by the disquieting sound of howling dogs. The remote sound sent shivers down his back, causing the hair on his neck to stand on end. There was no time to squander; soon the posse would be hot on his trail.

The pack of bloodhounds rapidly picked up the prisoner's odor, and the hunt was on. He hastily sprang to his feet and headed north through the woods. The weight of the chains hindered his getaway, and he lost ground to his pursuers. The violent howling of the dogs grew closer and closer, as the unrelenting echo constantly reminded him of the danger he was in. Attempting to elude the advancing posse, he jumped into a small stream, hopeful it would weaken his scent that the dogs clung to. Claiming early conquest, letting down his guard, he emerged from the stream to discover he was completely encircled, with no escape.

As I watched this movie, the thought came to me: God wants to free us from the chains of sin shackled to our lives. Sin leads us in wrong directions, slows us down, and will eventually encircle us with no escape. We can make every effort humanly possible to break free, but it will ultimately lead us to physical and mental exhaustion. There is only one way we can break free from these chains of sin, and run the race God has designed for us. Acts 3:19 says: "Repent, then, and turn to God, so that your sins may be wiped out, that times of refreshing may come from the Lord."

What has you bound, entangled, and exhausted? Is it the shackles of greed, envy, lying, thieving, alcohol abuse, drug abuse, sexual impurity, jealously, murder, adultery, anger, idolatry, slanderer, swindling? Is the sin in your life overbearing and digging into your conscience? There is a very straightforward solution to the problem. Jesus Christ holds the key and can unshackle the sin in our life and free us. Let us ask Jesus Christ to eradicate the shackles of sin today, tomorrow, and forever! Then run the race God has for us, and never worry about the posse again!

Lord Jesus,

Thank You for being a forgiving Lord, wanting to free us from the shackles of sin in our lives. We know You hold the key that can unlock the shackles and give us a new start. I pray we would examine our lives and discover the sin that has us bound, entangled, and exhausted, then drag our chains to You, knowing you can set us free and restore our strength in you.

"Abused Gifts"

Romans 12:6-8

"We have different gifts, according to the grace given us. If a man's gift is prophesying, let him use it in proportion to his faith. If it is serving, let him serve; if it is teaching, let him teach; If it is encouraging, let him encourage; if it is contributing to the needs of others, let him give generously; if it is leadership, let him govern diligently; if it is showing mercy, let him do it cheerfully." – NIV

It was my fourth birthday, and my Uncle Charlie gave me my first set of golf clubs. I also received an Indian chief outfit, headdress, and war paint. The excitement built inside me as I shoveled the last bite of cake and ice cream down my throat. I grabbed all my new stuff and darted out the front door. Golf clubs in one hand, Indian headdress in the other, I couldn't decide what to play with first. My mom followed me out with the remaining pieces of my Indian outfit. She helped me put on my costume and headdress then placed a couple of marks across my cheeks and forehead with red paint, as she wanted to take a picture before I ruined everything. I refused to give up my golf clubs, so the picture was taken of an excited little Indian playing golf.

At that age, my attention span was very short, so golfing only lasted a couple of minutes before my attention was drawn toward a new interest. Feathers and leather streaming down my back, war paint on my face, I grabbed a plastic club from my golf bag and proceeded to hunt the neighbor's pet. My uncle and parents had taken their eyes off me for a second, quickly finding me screaming like a rampant Indian on the warpath to scalp a cat. The cat didn't know what to presume, with ears folded back, and eyes watching my every move. I rapidly approached my victim, swinging my club, and just missed as the cat scurried across the lawn and up the nearest tree. I had never seen a cat move so fast, and continued to pursue my victim.

My parents chased after me screaming, "No, Brian, do not hit the cat! Do you hear us, young man? Do not hit that cat!" They quickly caught up with me and stripped the club from my hand. My mom said, "The battle is over young man!" Looking at her with my stern warrior face, I replied, "But Mom, I hadn't made my kill yet."

My parents had to educate me on what golf clubs were used for and not used for, and they explained cats were not created to be scalped, but were God's creation and needed to be loved and appreciated. My cat chasing days were over, and my golf clubs were taken away until I learned to respect and not abuse the gifts given to me.

The Lord gives gifts to his children to be used for his glory, yet at times, I have abused what was given to me and used it for a different purpose. We can become so eager to use our gifts and talents, and easily get sidetracked, abusing them for all the wrong reasons. The gifts and talents God designed us with from birth were designed for a precise purpose, to be used to bring glory to the Creator. The Lord allows us to make up our own mind on how we are to use what He has given us, and if we abuse the gifts, eventually we will be caught and will receive loving correction from our Father. God desires we use the talents and gifts He blessed us with to expand the Kingdom of God and bring glory to Him alone.

I have heard of Christians leaving high-paying careers and proceeding to take positions in the mission field, using the same talents or gifts and altering their careers to do something completely different. I read about a very successful lawyer losing his practice to pastor a church, and a successful surgeon who left his career for the mission field to operate on patients with cleft palates. Why do people do this? Do you feel you are using your talents and gifts for God's glory, and for furthering the Kingdom? I ask myself that very question as I write this. I am not saying we should quit our jobs and rush to the mission field, or start a whole new career, I am saying everything we do, including using our talents and gifts, need to honor Jesus Christ and nothing else. Let's ask ourselves, "What are the talents and gifts God has given us, and are we using them for the right purpose, or are we abusing our gifts?

Lord Jesus,

Thank You for Your mercy, grace, and love. Thank You for blessing each one of us with talents and gifts. I pray we would take a closer look at our lives and ask ourselves who we are glorifying ... You, or self? I pray everything we do, including using our talents, would bring honor only to You.

"Breath of Life"

Genesis 2:7

"Then the Lord God formed man from the dust of the ground and breathed into his nostrils the breath or spirit of life, and the man became a living being." [1 Cor. 15:45-49.] – AMP

John 20:21-22

"Again Jesus said, 'Peace be with you! As the Father has sent me, I am sending you.' And with that he breathed on them and said, 'Receive the Holy Spirit.'- NIV

I attended a "Wild at Heart" conference last fall, and part of the agenda was to spend time alone with God after each session. Time in the wilderness, detaching from the world. It was just what I needed to draw me closer to God. The morning session let out, and we were instructed to find a quiet place alone with God to discuss some specific questions we wrote down. Before leaving my chair, I closed me eyes for a moment, and an image of a blazing fire penetrated my mind, drawing me to the hill where we had a bonfire the night before. Trudging through wet leaves, slipping in the thick mud, I made my way up the hill to the fire pit.

The ground was waterlogged from the previous nights of hammering rain, and the once-roaring fire we all enjoyed was now a puddle of sodden ashes. Grabbing a chair close by, wiping the accumulated water off the seat, I sat down. In silence, I could feel short gusts of wind sweep past me, rousing the wet leaves on the ground, and I heard intervals of the lingering raindrops from leaves on the overhead trees striking the ground in a melody pleasing to the soul. I could instantaneously since the presence of God falling all around me. There was such a peace about being there in the midst of all the wetness.

I closed my eyes and began to pray, asking God the question I wrote from the session. "How have you awakened me, God, to what things you have awakened in my heart?" God directed me to gaze into the fire pit of wet, useless ashes. I aimed my attention there and saw nothing of use, saying to myself, "There is nothing here but a soggy mess, Lord." He instructed me through the Spirit to take a stick and stir around the wet ashes. Feeling silly, in obedience, I grabbed the closest branch and started to poke at the water-saturated pit. I was just about ready to give up and call it quits.

On my knees in amazement, closely inspecting the bed of ashes, eyes opened wide, I discovered a glowing ember, barely clinging to life. It would glow with each gust of wind passing by, but only smoldered, not strong enough to emit a flame. The Spirit of God told me to build around the ember and trust Him, but impatience got the best of me, so taking things into my own hands, I decided to blow on the ember. With each breath released from the full capacity of my lungs, I could only get the ember to glow a little brighter, but still no flame. My efforts resulted in exhaustion and frustration. Giving up, I said to myself, "It is no use."

In my conscience, God said to me, "Are you done Brian? Are you ready to trust Me as your source of your strength? Remember, I breathed life into you." Listening to God, with some doubt looming in my mind, I placed small twigs in the muddy ashes, bordered the twigs with wet newspaper, and constructed a medium-sized teepee around the smoldering ember. I sat back down in my chair and looked at the structure, thinking, "This is crazy, there is no way that wet mess will light, but I will give the whole thing to God in prayer." I closed my eyes again and said, "Lord, I am sorry, I give this to You and trust You with the outcome. Thank You for teaching me through this. Amen."

Moments later, a huge, continuous gust of wind arose over the hill. It was so strong, wet leaves were being lifted in the air, and I had to conceal my face from flying debris and ash. After a few seconds had passed and the wind calmed down, I opened my eyes. Glancing towards the fire pit, I noticed smoke, and where there is smoke, there is fire. The unresponsive ember had ignited the wet paper and twigs, bringing forth a flickering flame. I couldn't believe my eyes. Jumping out of my seat, I got down on my knees to assist the fire. God instructed me to not blow on the flame but build around it, and claim the victory of a roaring fire.

Within a half hour, the once-lifeless ember had been transformed into a small flame, and as I built around the fire, everything began to ignite, producing a revived fire. Summarized notes from that day: "Now as I write this, there is again a roaring fire and with each gust of wind, the fire now grows larger and stronger. God is showing me the waterlogged fire pit as my heart after the storm of divorce. I am barely clinging to God's Word and the glowing ember I stirred up is the remaining hope in me. The breath of God, where the wind wants to reach in me and ignite that hope in Him, and rekindle that once strong all-consuming fire of his Spirit living in my heart. He has shown me that my fire is not out and that He wants the fire in me to burn strong with every breath from Him, allowing my fire to become more intense.

Do you feel like a useless, burned-out ember, sitting in a pool of mud? We have to claim the victory of a burning fire by trusting and putting our faith in God. Those who have received the Holy Spirit have a strong, never-fading fire burning in them, waiting to be unleashed for God's glory. The day we were born, God breathed life into our body, and the day we accepted Christ, God filled us with the life of the Holy Spirit. We have the breath of life in us and we cannot allow the storms in our lives to extinguish the fire in us. God wants to rekindle that ember of hope in our hearts with one breath. We need to allow His breath to ignite the fire in us, to burn bright for Jesus. You may be saying, "All there is here is a sodden mess, Lord." God does not see a soggy mess, He sees what He created, and He wants to raise a smoldering ember into a roaring fire.

God wants His children to have life abundantly. He desires for us to be a fire for His Kingdom, and hates to see smoldering embers. Jesus sent the Holy Spirit to give us the power to do greater things than He did, through His name, and to be our comforter and guide through the storms. God wants us to claim His promises for us, and live obedient to His Word. Do you feel a stick stirring you or poking at you? That is God poking at your heart, seeking that burning ember, and wanting to blow on it to restore the roaring fire in your heart. Stop trying to do it yourself, look to God as the only source, and expect an invigorated fire to warm your soul.

Lord Jesus,

Thank You for giving all who accept You as their Lord and Savior the breath of the Holy Spirit. Thank you for continuing to blow the breath of life in us each day, knowing our hope is in You, and the fire burning in our hearts only grows stronger when we allow you to have control. I pray we would know we were designed to be a bright burning fire for You, and we would not allow the storms that come into our lives to extinguish the flame in our hearts.

"Called to Battle"

1 Samuel 17:45

David said to the Philistine, "You come against me with sword and spear and javelin, but I come against you in the name of the Lord Almighty, the God of the armies of Israel, whom you have defiled. This day the Lord will hand you over to me, and I'll strike you down and cut off your head. Today I will give the carcasses of the Philistine army to the birds of the air and the beasts of the earth, and the whole world will know that there is a God in Israel. All those gathered here will know that it is not by sword or spear that the Lord saves; for the battle is the Lord's, and he will give all of you into our hands."
- NIV

God called an ordinary man to battle, a man God had been molding and shaping into the warrior He was intended to become. The Bible describes David as being youthful, ruddy, and of fair countenance. The Lord called Samuel to anoint the next king, and in the process of selection, God told Samuel, "Do not consider his appearance or his height, for I have rejected him. The Lord does not look at the things man looks at. Man looks at the outward appearance, but the Lord looks at the heart." All seven of David's brothers passed before Samuel and were rejected. One son of Jesse remained, but surely David would not be chosen as king, he was just a young shepherd.

David was anointed in front of his seven brothers and received the Spirit of the Lord in power. The same Spirit of power lives within us as Christians. David possessed a faith like no other man, and was chosen by God to reveal his faith by facing a mountain of a man, a Philistine named Goliath. How did David come to master this inconceivable faith no other Israelite possessed, not even King Saul? How can we master faith and have no fear or hesitation when called to battle? David believed nothing could overcome the Lord in His power, and we must possess the same mindset.

Prior to David facing Goliath, his faith was being molded a couple of different times, when a bear and a lion took a lamb from the flock he was responsible for. David said, "I went out after him, and smote him, and delivered it out of his mouth." What would cause a man to chase after a lion or a bear? I personally have experienced a black bear up close, and wanted nothing to do with him. I have also seen shows depicting what a lion can do to its prey. David possessed a strong faith in the Lord, and he had to step into that faith to experience the power of the Spirit living within him. We will be molded and tested in our faith, and the most important thing we must do is be willing to pursue the bear or lion without hesitation or fear, knowing our strength is in the Lord.

The Philistine was nothing in David's eyes. David said to Saul the king, "Let no one lose heart on account of this Philistine; your servant will go and fight him." David's faith was so strong he knew if the Lord could deliver a lion and bear into his hands, the Philistine would be no different. David believed the entire army would be delivered into his hands by the Lord. He was willing to take on thousands of men with no fear, because he knew where his power stemmed from. I know we possess the same power, but I think I would hesitate to stand before a giant, let alone a whole army. David was so confident, he only took a staff, sling, and five stones into battle. Can you imagine what all the Israelites and Philistines were thinking when David stepped onto the battlefield? We need to possess that same confidence when facing the giants standing in our path.

Goliath said, "Am I a dog that you come at me with sticks?" Here stood a hardened warrior with many kills, reputed to be the strongest Philistine in the land. A champion covered in bronze armor, standing nine feet tall, and carrying a bronze javelin slung on his back. The Lord chose to use what seemed impossible to man to become possible, so all would see and believe there was a God in Israel. The Lord still uses that today, so in our weakness we know where our strength comes from. The only training David had was his faith experiences with God. Just as David, we have the strength of the Lord, and we can do all things through the name of Jesus Christ. Each battle we face is designed to bolster our faith in God.

David took a stone from his pouch and placed it in his sling. He hastened to meet this Philistine. He slung the stone and relied upon God for direction. The stone embedded into the giant's forehead, and Goliath fell upon his face, dead, to the earth. It only took one stone to drop a giant of a problem. When we are facing the giants in our lives, we must remember it only took an obedient servant to throw a single stone and trust the Lord with everything else. God knew exactly where that stone was destined, and all David had to do was be willing to be used as God's instrument in battle. David stepped out in faith, and God exalted him. If we endeavor to take on the giant problems in our own strength, we will collapse in defeat. But if we face our giants with faith in our hearts and know the battle is the Lord's, then we will walk away victorious!

Lord Jesus,

Today I pray that all my brothers and sisters in Christ would know You are their strength and stronghold. I pray we would remember to boldly step out in battle, trusting You with the outcome. We thank You, Lord, for the victory we have through the blood of Jesus Christ, and I pray that the Holy Spirit would give us the wisdom and discernment we will need in the battles to come.

"Calming the Storm"

Luke 8:22-24

"One day Jesus said to his disciples, 'Let's go over to the other side of the lake.' So they got into the boat and set out. As they sailed, Jesus fell asleep. A squall came down on the lake, so that the boat was being swamped, and they were in great danger. The disciples went and woke him, saying, 'Master, Master, we're going to drown!' He got up and rebuked the wind and the raging waters; the storm subsided, and all was calm." - NIV

Observing the faces of the people who went through Katrina, I saw them registering hopelessness, disbelief, uncertainty, and some having total peace. I can't imagine what people were thinking when Katrina took them by force, devastating everything in its path. I envision they were like the disciples being overpowered by the raging storm on the lake. Crying for someone to save them, full of fear, looking death in the face as the pounding waters overtook the cities. The aftermath speaks volumes, and there are those still trying to bounce back from being thrown face down in the mud.

Personally, I have never experienced a storm like Katrina, and hope I never will. It brings to mind a commercial on TV about butter, and the tag line was "Don't mess with Mother Nature!" I have witnessed footage of some storms full of death and destruction. Watching the clips, I find myself drawn to the force of a tornado, hurricane, or typhoon, as my eyes fasten onto its devastating path of destruction. Trees snapped like toothpicks, vehicles tossed like base-balls, and the remains of houses scattered like spilt sugar, all signs of a rampaging storm. The disciples focused on the storm instead of listening to the voice of their Master when He told them, "Let's go over to the other side of the lake."

We will encounter Katrinas in life, and we can either let the storm annihilate us, leaving a path of destruction and aftermath, or we can rely upon something much stronger than any storm we'll ever face. On the boat with the disciples, Jesus stretched out his hand, commanding the storm to be quiet, and calmed the sea. Can you visualize experiencing that? The disciples, in fear and amazement, asked one another, "Who is this? He commands even the wind and the water, and they obey him." One moment, you feel like you are going to die, gasping for the breath of life, and in a moment you are observing clear skies and calm seas. What power we have through the name of Jesus! We must trust in the Lord and know He will get us through the storm to the other side of the lake.

Oral Roberts said it best, and I hope this encourages you as much it did me, to invite Jesus into your boat before the storm hits. He said, "The storms of life come to everybody - to the saved, and unsaved, to those who live in God's will and to those who don't. The only difference is that Jesus is in the Christian's boat just like he was with the disciples, and that makes all the difference in the world."

If you suffer from the waves of adversity pounding on your hull, or the waters of oppression pouring into your boat, don't panic. Stop fearing, and in faith call out to Jesus, asking Him to quiet the storm in your life. Remember, He may keep us in the storm awhile, but He will always get us through and to the other side. Jesus wants to ride in our boats and be our strength in our weakness. In His name, we have the power to calm the raging storms. Always remember, Jesus is bigger and more powerful than anything we will sail through in life.

Lord Jesus,

Thank You for being our strength in the storm, promising never to leave us nor forsake us, and always bringing us out of the storms safely. Thank You for the power we have in Your name, the power to calm a raging storm. I pray we would all invite You into our boats and trust You with our lives as we sail day to day with You. I pray the storms would not bring us into fear or confusion, but peace, knowing we are only going to be wet for a little while.

"Commander in Chief"

Hebrews 11:7

[Prompted] by faith, Noah, being forewarned by God concerning events of which as yet there was no visible sign, took heed and diligently and reverently constructed and prepared an ark for the deliverance of his own family. By this [his faith which relied on God] he passed judgment and sentence on the world's unbelief and became an heir and possessor of righteousness (that relation of being right into which God puts the person who has faith). [Gen. 6 13-22.]
– AMP

Visualize with me for a moment passing by your neighbor's house, noticing the beginning stages of construction. We may think, "Hey, what is our neighbor doing? That sure is a lot of wood in his front yard." Each day passing the house, we notice the development taking shape and we continue to speculate on what the heck our neighbor is building. Peering through our windows, we notice him working day and night on this project. What could be so important that an individual would dedicate their every waking hour to? We ask our neighbors if they knew what was going on, and we listen for the latest developing rumors.

What was Noah thinking? He might have thought, "Lord, all my neighbors are staring at me like I'm crazy and they are beginning to ask questions. Should I tell them?" No matter what was said, Noah did not allow anything to divert him from completing the task God commanded him to do. Notice I said, "God commanded Noah." He did not ask him to build the ark. God said, "Make yourself an ark of gopher wood; make in it rooms (stalls, pens, coops, nests, cages, and compartments) and cover it inside and out with pitch (bitumen)." Gen. 6:14 - AMP God was preparing a way for the new covenant for us, and he commanded an ordinary man to get the job done. I bet Noah faced some antagonism and mockery as he obeyed God and built the ark. Noah did not ask any questions, he just did what he was commanded to do.

What would our reaction be if Noah lived in our neighborhood and was building an ark in his yard? Like me, would you watch him in skepticism as he put the concluding touches on his mountain of wood? We might have said, "Hey, that sure is a large wooden box you got there, Noah, and why do you have living creatures invading our neighborhood?" Come on, how would you have reacted if you witnessed animals lining up for miles, boarding this large wooden crate your neighbor built? I imagine the whole world labeled Noah as being crazy, but what did they think when the floodwaters started to rise and they saw the ark float away?

The Lord, our Commander in Chief, commands us to do things for the Kingdom, and we must be willing to do anything He calls us to do, no matter how crazy it may seem. We cannot be concerned with what our neighbors say as we pile the wood in our front yards, build our arks, and invite all the animals to our neighborhood. We have to stay focused on God's command and plan. We may have to work day and night to complete the task and we cannot let opposition or ridicule stop us. We must be prepared to accept people staring, laughing, and mocking us as we step out of our comfort zone and do what God has commanded.

What has God commanded you to do, and have you picked up your hammer yet? He has a perfect plan for each one of us, and we have to be obedient to his command in our lives. Are we prepared to be a Noah, an ordinary man, listening to the command, following the plan, and becoming an extraordinary man? Noah did not allow anything to get in the way of completing what God called him to do. What a role model we have. What is stopping us today? Are we afraid of what our neighbors may think or what the world may think? We need to complete the task before the Lord returns. Upon his return, I desire the Lord to see me holding my hammer and building my ark. How about you?

Lord Jesus,

Thank You for using ordinary people to do extraordinary things. Thank You for giving us a purpose and plan. You are our Commander in Chief, and I pray we would hear your command and pick up our hammers, letting nothing stop us from building the ark.

"Double-Minded?"

1 Corinthians 15:48

"Now those who are made of the dust are like him who was first made of the dust (earthly-minded); and as is [the Man] from heaven, so also [are those] who are of heaven (heavenly-minded)." - AMP

I was invited out to dinner with some friends, and upon being seated after a long wait, the waitress introduced herself, listed the house specials, then asked, "Are you folks ready to order?" After a positive reply, she started at the opposite end of the table, scratching her pen on paper. I scanned over the menu, but nothing seemed to grab my appetite. Everyone knew exactly what they wanted, as if the menu was photocopied in their minds. Soon the waitress was breathing down my neck, eyes on me, and asked, "And for you sir?" I could not make up my mind and was holding up the entire order. I replied, "Can you give me a few more moments please?" I could sense the entire table wishing I would hurry up and make up my mind.

Frustrated, as the pressure was building, I raced through the menu again, hoping the waitress would be delayed. Thinking about several different entrées, trying to decide which one would be the best selection, I narrowed my decision. I could hear the growls of hunger as my friends patiently waited for the waitress to return and complete our order. I noticed the waitress heading back to our table, and I felt the cold stare from her beaming down on me as I hesitated but completed my order. The moment she disappeared from sight, I immediately thought, "I should have chosen the other entree."

I share this story to illustrate being double-minded. It is so easy for our minds to be filled with anxiety, worry, envy, and fear. We first allowed something negative to penetrate our thinking, then we focused our minds on Christ to remove the negative thought, but soon we find our minds focusing on the negative thoughts again. For example, we may worry about how we are going to make enough money to pay all our bills, then read in the Bible the Lord will supply all our needs according to his will, but find ourselves overwhelmed with doubtful thinking when the bills begin to stack up and due dates approach quickly. God wants us to be covenant-minded, not double-minded. You may be asked, what is being covenant-minded?

A covenant with God means joining with Him to gain His strength, His authority, His name, His weapons and His power. If we focus our minds on this covenant He made with us, there is no room for being double-minded, because it does not reflect the promise He made to us in His Word. We have to start thinking with this covenant on our minds. We are joint heirs to Jesus Christ the moment we accept Him as our Lord and Savior. When Jesus died for us, He was knit with our souls through his blood. This blood covenant represents God's love for us, meaning no matter what happens and no matter how little we give to Him in return, we will forever be at the forefront of God's thinking.

Being covenant-minded is not allowing anything negative to enter into our minds, and standing on God's Word in our daily thinking. We can transform our minds by focusing on godly things and avoid what does not reflect God's promises to us. We have to learn to trust in the things we cannot see, and not worry about the stack of bills staring us in the face. We have to trust in God's Word, and not be moved by what we see, but know in our minds we are covered in the blood of Jesus. God made a blood covenant with us. I always wondered why Jesus' words were written in red. Could it be his Words represent his blood covenant to us?

The next time we find our minds racing from one thing to another and we sense doubt, fear, envy, or worry, cry out, "Jesus, cleanse our minds with your blood!" Remember, breaking away from the covenant will lead us to confusion and sin, but repentance will place us back in the blood again. We need to ask ourselves "Does my thinking line up with God's Word?" Being covenant-minded will increase our faith in God's Word. Being double-minded will only lead to being tossed in the sea of being unable to make up our minds, and drowning in negativity. Covenant faith stands, and we do not have to wonder about our faith, because we stand with God in the blood!

Lord Jesus,

Thank You for the covenant we have in Your blood. Thank You, Lord, we have the power in Your name to overcome being double-minded. I pray we would focus on the covenant You made with us on the cross, and we would stand strong on Your promises you give us in Your Word. I pray we would honor the covenant we have with You through our actions, words, and thoughts, and we would never allow negativity to penetrate our minds.

"Don't Give Up"

Psalms 18:32-33

"The God who girds me with strength and makes my way perfect; He makes my feet like hinds' feet [able to stand firmly or make progress on the dangerous heights of testing and trouble]; He sets me securely upon high places." – AMP

The pain was unbearable, and my mind throbbed with signals to stop. Taking a mouthful of water and consuming my last few gummy bears, I was determined to attain the energy needed to finish the climb. The heaviness of the backpack put stress on my knees, shins, and ankles as we continued the difficult ascent. The trail was uneven and rocky, and at times it seemed never-ending. I placed each of my steps with awareness, so I would not lose my foothold and cave in under the pressure of gravity. My body became numb with pain, and uncertainty was strong on my mind.

I had to muster up all my strength to climb the irregular stairway of rocks and crevasses. My calves were ready to explode, and my thighs were burning like an out-of-control forest fire. The burden was too much. Slowing my pace, I fell behind the other climbers. The climb became harder and my steps became slower and heavier. Taking my next step, I missed the ridge and lost my balance. The crushing weight of my backpack was forcing me to lunge forward. Trying to soften the fall, I reached for anything I could find, only to be grabbing air. The collapse sent me plummeting onto rocks, debris, and hard ground.

My backpacking partners heard the fall and rushed to my rescue. One of the climbers unfastened the hip and shoulder straps and lifted the seventy-five pound backpack from my sweaty back. Feeling the weight lifted off my back, I felt weightless, like a feather in the wind. Two other hikers grabbed me under the arms and propped me back up on my feet. I began to assess my body for any damage and bent over, sighing with a deep breath of relief. Legs still anesthetized with pain, right knee sore from the impact, I sat down, taking a few minutes to gain my strength back. A couple of hikers removed the contents of my backpack to help lessen the load so I could finish the ascent to our campsite. Despite everything that happened, I did not give up.

I have asked myself, "What if Jesus gave up?" What if He permitted the weight of the cross to overcome Him on his climb to Mount Calvary? The good news is that He did not give up, but instead took on the weight of the World's sin, both yours and mine, and carried it upon His flogged and bleeding back to His death. Jesus loves you and me so much that He sacrificed Himself so we could have the one and only way to His Father, so we could spend eternity with Him in heaven. Jesus' purpose on Earth was to become human, be empowered with the Spirit of God, and save all sinners who have fallen from the weight of sin in their lives.

God formed us with a specific purpose in mind, giving us gifts to carry out His will for our lives. What is your purpose in life? God says, "I know what I am planning for you ... I have good plans for you, not plans to hurt you. I will give you hope and a good future." I am not saying life is going to be unproblematic; just the opposite, life will be full of tests and challenges. There are going to be times when we feel like the crushing weight of the world is on our backs and we want to give up. The trail of life is not going to be a smooth path. It will be a stairway of rugged rocks and crevasses, and there will be times when we fall down exhausted and overwhelmed. Jesus will always be there to lift us up in His resurrected power, lighten the load, and give us the strength we need to reach our destination. Remember, our God is able to do far more than we can ever dare to ask or even dream of - infinitely beyond our highest prayers, desires, thoughts, or hopes.

Lord Jesus,

Thank You for being our friend, helper, and provider. You will always be with us on our journey in life. You will help us up when we lose our footing, when we call upon your name, and You will provide the strength we need in our weakness. I pray we would not give up when the weight of circumstances comes crushing down on us. Instead, we will keep our eyes focused on God's will for our lives and renew our strength daily in Christ to overcome any obstacle that may cause us to fall.

"Dying to be Rich"

1 Timothy 6:17

"As for the rich in this world, charge them not to be proud and arrogant and contemptuous of others, nor to set their hopes on uncertain riches, but on God, Who richly and ceaselessly provides us with everything for [our] enjoyment." - AMP

Fingers black with metallic residue, eyes glued to the rolling wheels, she continued to deposit coins into the slot machines. Hours had passed and she was down to her last few coins. She had been possessed with the fever of dying to get rich in Las Vegas. Pulling the handle, eyes opened wide, she waited with anticipation for the wheels to stop. Three sevens triggered the winning alarm, and lights flashed all around her. She exclaimed at the top of her lungs, after jumping from her seat, "Jackpot!" She shoveled handfuls of coins into a plastic bucket. Faster and faster her hands moved from the machine to the bucket, attentive not to miss one coin. As people began to huddle around her, she clung to the bucket as if were her life savings.

Do you realize this happens day and night in the world? People are dying to get rich any way they can. People are willing to do outrageous things for the almighty buck. I am sure you are aware of the hit TV show *Fear Factor*. For $50,000, selected contestants are required to face their worst fears, and complete gut-churning tasks like eating live worms. *Who Wants To Be a Millionaire*? is another popular show viewed by thousands. I can't help but wonder how many applicants apply and want a shot at making all their dreams come true. Billboards posted along our highways show us the latest statistics for the lottery, getting us to think like millionaires. People standing in line, clenching their tickets in hand, perceiving they have picked the winning numbers, and planning what they are going to do with the winnings.

The devil has a major foothold on our world, and most people have become blinded with "The Love of Money, the Root of All Evil" that surrounds us every day. It can take over as a god in our lives and we can become snared in worshiping our money and possessions. I knew a friend who washed and waxed his boat every week, and he built a custom garage to store it in. At times, I found myself wanting more money and things, but Jesus warns us about this in the parable of the rich young ruler. He said, "Watch out! Be on your guard against all kinds of evil; a man's life does not consist in abundance of his possessions." The world teaches just the opposite "The Boy Who Dies with The Most Toys Wins."

Is it really all about money? God knows what we need, and if it is according to His will, He will give us what we need, because it is all God's, anyway. We are to manage what the Lord gives us for the Lord's glory. Jesus said, "Seek ye first the Kingdom of God, and his righteousness, and these things will be added to you." Jesus wants us to build our treasures in heaven, because where our treasures are, there our hearts will be also. In Proverbs 23:4, we are warned again: "Do not wear yourself out to get rich; have the wisdom to show restraint. Cast but a glance at riches, and they are gone, for they will surely sprout wings and fly off to the sky like an eagle."

Each day, we need to pray for our daily bread, and God will provide just the right amount we need. He knows if we are given too much, and are not trustworthy with what He gives us, we may say, 'Who is the Lord?' Just like the rich fool who tore down his barns to make room for more, and thought to himself, "You have plenty of good things laid up for many years, so I will take life easy, eat, drink, and be merry." But God said, "You fool! This very night your life will be required of you, then who will get what you have prepared for yourself?" –AMP. God has the power to give or take as He pleases. He wants all His children to live abundant lives, but He does not want us to worship anything other than Him. There is nothing wrong with money and possessions, as long as we do not put them over God. Jesus Christ must to be first in our lives and we can trust the Lord that He will give us everything we need. Jesus Christ died on the cross for one reason, so we can have a personal relationship with God and receive the treasures of heaven.

I met some homeless people in Covington, KY. I was overwhelmed with what my eyes envisioned. These brothers and sisters were so appreciative to receive a warm cup of chili, and a cold cup of Kool-aid. I walked around with my Bible in hand, asking if I could pray for any needs they might have. Most of them professed a personal relationship with Jesus Christ. There was a man who shared his personal testimony with me. He felt the Lord was using him to minister to other homeless people in a special way, and he said, "All I need in life, Brian, is Jesus, he has provided me with everything I need and has always given me plenty." After praying together, he reached out his hand and shook mine saying, "I have lost everything, I have no earthly possessions, but now I am building treasures in heaven."

Where are we building our treasures? Are we storing treasure up for ourselves, or are we building treasures in heaven? The Lord gives every man and women a gift to use for His glory, and He wants us to use those gifts to further His Kingdom. Do we know what gift or gifts we possess? If not, ask God to reveal those to us, so we can begin to store up treasures that will never fly away like an eagle. No jackpot, lottery, or winnings will ever compare to what we can have in a personal relationship with Jesus Christ. Instead of dying to be rich, we should be thankful our riches are found in Christ. So let's wash the black residue from our fingers, take our eye off the spinning wheels, stop trying to become rich overnight, and start trusting in Jesus to provide us with our daily bread.

Lord Jesus,

Thank You for providing everything we need and for giving us the desires of our hearts. Thank You for Your Word and for the promises it brings to us. I pray we would wash our hands of the black residue, stop trying to get rich overnight, and place our trust in the source and supply that never fades away. I pray we would not get caught up in the world system of gaining wealth, but we would start using the resources You provide for us to further the Kingdom and build treasures in heaven.

"Answering the Call"

ⳬ

Romans 11:29

"For God's gifts and His call are irrevocable. [He never withdraws them when once they are given, and He does not change His mind about those to whom He gives His grace or to whom He sends His call.]" - AMP

Immediately after stepping off the bus from my long trip from Arizona, I was pulled in a hundred different directions, preparing for my long stay in New Jersey. Standing in several long lines, collecting different items, I finally finished the processing. The long night had come to an end and I dragged my exhausted, limp body to bed. The surroundings were all new to me and the bed was not as comfortable as my bed at home, but out of pure fatigue, I quickly fell asleep.

It only had been a few hours since my head hit the pillow, when suddenly I was awakened from a loud crash of a trash can hitting an adjacent wall. A loud, boisterous voice echoed through the dark silent room, "Get out of your bunks, soldiers, and fall into formation!" It sounded like my alarm clock at home, and I had been used to reaching over and hitting the snooze button, thus ignoring the early wake-up call from the drill sergeant.

I felt heavy breathing in my face and heard a soft voice whisper, "Do you want me to get you up in an hour or so, Mr. Steenhoek?" My groggy reply was, "Yes, can you let me sleep in a little longer please." Several moments of silence passed, and thinking my request had been granted, I slipped back to sleep. I felt the mattress under me lift and bow like a camel's back, and I quickly discovered how the mattress under me could fly through the air after being tossed from the upper bunk to the cold hard floor. I found myself standing in my boxers in front of the company's commander, explaining why I failed to follow orders on the first day of basic training, resulting in not getting up on time with the rest of my platoon.

There are times when the Lord calls us and we tend to reach over and hit the snooze buttons in our minds, thinking we can use a few more minutes of sleep or ignore the call completely. When God calls our name, we cannot afford to put off our response or ignore His call on our lives. We might find ourselves lying prostrate on the floor after the Lord gets our attention. We are all called to be soldiers in Christ's Army, and to react to His call in our lives at any moment's notice. We can choose to immediately respond, donning our armor, grabbing our sword, and showing up for battle. Or we can respond late, resulting in us standing in our skivvies, not prepared, and explaining why we are not ready to do what He has called us to do.

We can try to avoid the call altogether by hiding in our caves of unresponsiveness, but what good is that? The Lord will get our attention eventually. Just look how he got Jonah's attention after placing him in the belly of a fish for a few days. We need to awake immediately to the Lord's call on our lives and not delay a moment, because if we do, we could miss the most important battle of our lives. I desire the Lord to see me with my sword in hand, standing on the battlefield, answering His call. How about you? Will you respond to God's call in your life and stand with me in what could be the greatest battle of our lives?

Lord Jesus,

Thank You for giving us the armor of God. I pray we would not hit the snooze button when You call, but would jump to attention, don our armor and sword, and show up for battle. I pray we would not fear anything and come out of our caves, knowing the victory is ours, given by Your hand.

"First or Last?"

Matthew 16:26

"For what is a man profited, if he shall gain the whole world, and lose his own soul? Or what shall a man give in exchange for his soul?" - NKJ

Mark 9:35

"If any man desire to be first, the same shall be last of all, and servant to all."- NKJ

Poised and ready, weapon loaded, I prepared for the release of the target. The florescent orange disk launched in front of me and I quickly took aim, lining the sight on the barrel to the target, and squeezed the trigger. The shotgun went off and I soon realized the target continued on its path untouched. I had missed the disk, and frustration immediately set in.

My second try soon arrived. I was looking forward to success as I loaded the shotgun and anticipated the release of the clay disk. I took my position and shouted, "Pull!" as I gazed down the sight. The disk whipped across the sky. Quickly taking aim, I squeezing off a round, missing again! The frustration escalated, as I thought, "What is wrong with you, Brian? You better get your act together, or you will come in last." We all started talking about who was the better shot and this joking ramble soon led to a competition between us shooters.

The third attempt was looking me straight in the face and the pressure of being the best shot was really beginning to get to me. Loading the shotgun for a third time, I prepared to fire. This time, I hit the target and was able to take the lead over the other shooters.

It has always been my nature to be number one and nothing less. I have always felt there was no place for second in my book, and tend to be hard on myself when I fail to be first. I hit the most targets, and in the midst of my personal private celebration, the Lord told me in my spirit, "It is not about being first, Brian, but has everything to do with being last." My thinking was, "But Lord, that's against my nature!" The Lord put the above scripture passage in my heart and gave me something to think about as we returned to the cabin.

The Lord wants us to put others before ourselves, to see others as more valuable, and to love others as we love ourselves. Why is this so difficult to do? I know it has everything to do with Christ's love inside us. If we seek the love of Jesus with all our hearts, minds and souls, then His love will spill out of us to others like gushing water. His love in us will also burn away anything that does not belong in our hearts. I am learning it is all about a personal, loving relationship with the Christ within us. That is the starting point to overcoming our selfish desire to be number one in this world.

I used to hate to see others more successful than me, but that is changing because the Lord is teaching me His love is all I need to gain, and seeking his love first will lead me to sharing His love with others. If you are struggling with this, please take these words to heart. I am also learning by putting others first, and you can experience a different kind of success in Christ. The Christ in us is the most important thing we can gain and profit from while on this earth.

Lord Jesus,

Thank You for Your words of conviction. Thank You for living in our hearts, filling us with Your love, and for using us to spread your love to this world. I pray we would seek the Christ in us and allow Your love to destroy all our selfish desires, and teach us to put others before ourselves.

"Follow Me"

Proverbs 21:21

"He who earnestly seeks after and craves righteousness, mercy, and loving-kindness will find life in addition to righteousness (uprightness and right standing with God) and honor." - AMP

Can you imagine dropping everything you had to follow Jesus Christ? Jesus said, "Follow me," and immediately the disciples left everything to follow after righteousness. Peter left his material possessions, John left his father, and Matthew left his career; all to follow something that stole their attention.

Dropping everything, asking no questions, they stepped out in faith, took nothing with them, and trusted Jesus, who they just met moments ago. I wonder what was going through their minds and did they ever have second thoughts? It had to be a very powerful influence to get them to leave everything they had to follow a man on a mission from God.

I don't know how I would have responded if I was called to follow Jesus, how about you? "What about my personal obligations and commitments? Who will take care of everything while I'm gone? Could I have a few days to think it over?" I think these would have been some of my questions in response to His command, "Follow me."

I am not condoning anyone leaving employment, family, or possessions to follow Jesus. I am stating, "He still commands us and we are faced with a choice. His Word tells us to pick up our crosses daily and follow Him. When the cross is in your hands, there is no room for anything else, and we need to put Him at the head of our lives, following after his righteousness and mercy." Nothing we have is more important than our relationship with the Lord. But why do we at times put Him on the back burner, only to be used in case of an emergency?

What trust the disciples had in Jesus. Leaving everything, they trusted Jesus with all aspects of their lives. I find it very difficult to surrender one area of my life over to Jesus, let alone everything. The Lord wants to be present in all areas of our lives, not some...all. He is patient with us and will eventually get all our attention. Our faith and trust must be like the disciples', leaving everything in God's hands. No matter what the circumstance, standing on the Word of God, and trusting in the one who gives us life.

Jesus wants to show the light, the truth, and the life to all who will follow Him. The disciples needed nothing more than Jesus their whole lives. You will see all but one of the disciples found life, righteousness, and honor. These three characteristics should be our goal in life. First, we must seek Jesus' face daily, we must pick up our cross and chase after His righteousness and mercy, and we must honor the Lord with all our actions, words, and thoughts.

Like me, what are you still holding on to? I have a fear of letting go, thinking only of the negative to come from it. But Jesus is telling me to hand it over to Him, as He wants to lighten my load. He is telling you the same thing. The more we hang onto, the more difficult it will be to carry our crosses. We were designed for one thing: to be in fellowship with God through His Son, Jesus Christ. Jesus is calling us to follow Him and not worry about our lives. He has everything under control, and just like the disciples, we will need nothing more than Him. So allow Jesus to steal your attention, drop all your nets, lighten your loads, and pick up your crosses.

Lord Jesus,

Thank You for being the light and the ultimate source of life. Thank You for your promises in your Word that we can stand on and claim as ours. I pray we would put You first in all areas of our lives and put everything else second, then follow You with our crosses daily. I pray we would not hesitate when You call us and set the goal to chase after righteousness, and honor You with our lives.

"Fool's Gold"

1 John 4:1-3

"Dear friends, do not believe every spirit, but test the spirits to see whether they are from God, because many false prophets have gone out into the world. This is how you can recognize the Spirit of God: **Every spirit that acknowledges that Jesus Christ has come in the flesh is from God, but every spirit that does not acknowledge Jesus is not from God.** *This is the spirit of the antichrist, which you have heard is coming and even now is already in the world." –* NIV

B ent at my knees, water up to my ankles, I anxiously search for anything shiny. I carefully sifted through the mud and debris with my hands after shaking my pan several times. I was hoping to strike it rich by discovering gold. Pan after pan of muddy water, with nothing to show for my efforts. Some of the scouts had a few of us convinced we would find gold, and my heart was set on becoming a millionaire. I was one of the few scouts who did not understand the likelihood of discovering anything valuable would be low.

Our Boy Scout Troop had the opportunity to visit a mining area while camping, and pan for gold. A fellow scout was panning next to me, and when I was not paying attention, he placed a piece of fool's gold in my pan that he had purchased from the gift store prior to us getting started. I was getting discouraged with the whole mining thing until the sparkle caught my eye. A surge of energy shot through my body like a bolt of lightning. My heart began racing as I quickly brushed away the sandy mud to discover gold!

I proclaimed with a loud voice, "I'm rich! I'm rich! I found gold!" I nearly broke my leg exiting the creek, racing to the guide who instructed us to come to him with any discovery. I handed him my small piece of gold and anxiously waited to hear his reply. He carefully examined the rock and a large smile came across his face. I responded with a smile and my eyes grew to the size of golf balls. By this time, most of the scouts had gathered to see the new discovery, including the scout who had tricked me. The guide played along for a few minutes and had me convinced I had discovered real gold.

Then my bubble of excitement was popped like a balloon when he told me it was gold, but fool's gold. At first I did not believe him, as I thought he was out to steal my claim. The scout who tricked me confessed to placing it in my mining pan, and explained he was only doing it for fun. I truly thought it was gold, but soon discovered it was a fake. It resembled the real thing, but the quality was totally different. Later, we all had a great laugh at the campfire, and I learned a valuable lesson from the experience.

Before getting excited about anything now, I test it to see if it is the real thing. Several times, I have put things to the test to make sure I was getting the genuine article and not an imposter. I have discovered Jesus Christ is the genuine thing we can place our trust in and know everything else is an imposter. In your life, someone may place something in your pan and you may think it is the real thing, but carefully inspect and test it before jumping to your feet and rushing to show off your discovery. We could find ourselves chasing after something resembling the real thing, but eventually discovering a decoy in our pan.

The Scripture passage reminded me of that time in my life when I was too naive to understand the difference between gold and fool's gold. The Scripture also gives us a simple way to test if a spirit is of God or an imposter. If the spirit does not believe Jesus Christ came in the flesh from God, then it is not of God. These are the spirits we need to stay away from, because they will only lead us to fool's gold. We have to be careful and test everything to see if it is of God and not of our enemy. The devil can make things look very shiny and attractive to us, but beware of the things not of God. The things of God are genuine gold and hold more value than a dirty fake rock.

Lord Jesus

Thank You for being the one thing we can trust in and know everything about You is the truth. You are more valuable than gold and there is nothing fake about You. I pray we would compare everything to You and get rid of anything that does not match up with Your character or the Word of God. I pray we would be cautious about what we hear and see, as we only want the real thing, nothing fake.

"Freedom"

Galatians 5:1

"Stand fast therefore in the liberty wherewith Christ hath made us free, and be not entangled again with the yoke of bondage." – KJV

Freedom! The last word voiced by William Wallace before being beheaded, as played by Mel Gibson in the blockbuster movie, *Braveheart.* Why would one man go through so much for freedom, I ask myself. He wanted the best for the Scottish people, and William Wallace did not want the people sacrificing their freedom for slavery to England. William was willing to die a horrific death rather than kneel and confess his loyalty to the King of England. The English people spat upon him, mocked him, and hit him. I noticed during the whole process of his torture and death, he clung to the one thing that was keeping him alive, the scarf from his one true love, who was executed by the English.

Many soldiers have died fighting in several different wars to give us freedom to live in this country. This past Memorial Day, I stood in front of a WWII memorial, and in silence read the names of the men etched on the metal plate. I did not know them, yet they believed in freedom and gave their life so we could enjoy what we have today. Many of these men have been forgotten, as their names have faded into history. I imagine there were heroes we never heard about who performed courageous acts, believing in something driven deep in their hearts called Freedom.

There is another man I would like to introduce to you, who also died for our freedom. He wants the best for all his people and He was willing to die so we could be free for eternity. He was spat upon, mocked, and beaten. He clung to the two crossed beams, barely able to walk, and made a slow, painful journey toward Mount Calvary. There He was stretched out, nails were driven deep into His hands and feet, and He was raised for all to see what one man's heart was willing to do for freedom. He screamed with his last breath, "It is finished!" That penetrated the ears of the devil, signifying the devil's defeat. He died so we could have freedom and spend eternity with Him, not slaves to the devil forever.

His name is above all names and will never fade away because He is alive today. He wants to scribe His name on our hearts and live in us and through us. Do not forget what He did for us, and each time you look at the cross in silence, remember whose blood was shed there for us. So, ask Jesus to come into your heart, and claim your freedom today! He knows us by name and desires for all of us to come to Him, as He is the only way to Heaven.

Lord Jesus,

Thank You, Lord Jesus, for doing a bold and courageous act. Thank You for giving us a way to spend eternity with You. I pray Your death will not be in vain, and all of us who you know by name would look only to You for true Freedom. I pray for every living being on the face of this earth, please accept Jesus as your Lord and Savior before it is too late.

"I Promise?"

Psalm 105:8-10

"He hath remembered his covenant forever, the word which he commanded to a thousand generations. Which covenant he made with Abraham, and his oath to Isaac; And confirmed the same unto Jacob for a law, and to Israel for an everlasting covenant." - KJV

I have been seeking wisdom from the Lord, asking Him to show me through His Word the meaning of a covenant. Divinely, I received some information in the mail from a national ministry entitled "Covenant Made by Blood." I just started the study, and discovered some things in a covenant that has led me to write these thoughts.

Very excited to have received this information, I dove into the study, and I am beginning to understand what a blood covenant is. The covenant was taken very seriously, and the only way out was death. There were specific steps that took place, and I will briefly describe them so we can get a picture in our minds of how serious this act was.

The grounds for the covenant agreement were based on their differences, not their similarities. The two parties would then discuss each other's responsibilities and terms of the covenant. Then each party would choose a representative to display their strength in the union. A covenant site was picked, where all members of the parties could witness the ceremony. The sacrificial animal was selected, and most often it was an animal that would shed a great deal of blood.

The animal was cut from the neck down the backbone, so both halves would fall away from each other and the animal's blood and insides would drain between the two halves. This was called the alley of blood. Each representative would first remove his coat and exchange it with the other party. This represented strength and authority, and their weapon belts were exchanged, signifying joining in battle until death.

Then they would walk down the blood alley and stop between the two halves, standing ankle-deep in blood. They made irrevocable promises and stated the curse or penalty for breaking the promises. Each representative would cut their own flesh, usually the wrist or palm, then join hands, mingling their blood together under the witness of God. To stop the bleeding, they would rub a substance on the wound, which would leave a noticeable scar to remind them forever of what took place.

Finally, the two parties would join their two names together and exchange their friendship. All would sit down and partake of bread and wine, symbolizing each party's body and blood given to each other, then giving themselves to the other in eternal friendship.

Jesus died on the cross so we do not have to abide in the old covenant, but we are in a new blood covenant with Jesus Christ the moment we accept him as our Lord and Savior. Jesus died on the cross for you and me, and it was His blood that became the alley of blood. The moment Jesus died on the cross, the tabernacle and curtain was split in two, just like an animal being sacrificed. There was no more need for animal sacrifice, because the perfect sacrifice was made at Calvary.

The Lord handed us His coat of righteousness and the armor for protection. Jesus took nails in his hands and feet for us, leaving scars reminding him of what he did for us. Finally, He gave us His body and blood, the bread and wine, the final step of a blood covenant. At the Last Supper, He said "...this is my body, which is broken for you: this do in remembrance of me...This cup is the new testament in my blood: this do ye, as oft as you drink it, in remembrance of me" (1 Corinthians 11:24-25) - JKV

Some final things to think about:

Jesus took going to the cross very seriously, keeping His promises to us. He gave His best for us, are we giving our best to Him? He just wants to hold us in His blood and give us His righteousness and strength. What are you willing to give Him?

Lord Jesus,

Thank You for being the ultimate sacrifice, shedding Your innocent blood at Calvary. Thank You, God, for sacrificing Your Son, Jesus, so we can place our faith and trust in His blood and claim eternal life with You forever. I pray that we would take this covenant as seri-

ously as Jesus did when He went to the cross for us, and I pray that we would keep our promises and honor this covenant You provided for us.

"God, Where Are You!"

Romans 12:1-2

"I beseech you therefore, brethren, by the mercies of God, that ye present your bodies a living sacrifice, holy, acceptable unto God, which is your reasonable service. And be not conformed to this world: but ye transformed by the renewing of your mind, that ye may prove what is that good, and acceptable, and perfect, will of God." - KJV

At seventeen, I had a dream from God and He gave me a vision. I was the youngest of my brothers, and had a father who loved and favored me. My father had sent me to check on my brothers and my life changed that day. My beautiful coat was ripped from my back, my brothers grabbed me with force and shoved me in an empty, dark, deep cistern, and left me to die. Eventually, my brothers pulled me from the musty hole and handed me over to a group of strangers. I was sold for twenty pieces of silver and became a slave for an Egyptian master.

Life was looking up when my master promoted me to be head of his household, and everything I did prospered for a time, but again my life took a turn. I was thrown into prison for attempted rape, as all evidence pointed to my guilt. I was placed in charge of the prison, and again everything I did prospered there. I met a couple of prisoners from the palace and had the opportunity to interpret their dreams. They promised to tell their master, but again I was forgotten and left to rot in prison.

Several years later, I was called out of prison to interpret a dream for the head honcho of Egypt. God had given me the ability to explain these dreams in detail, and this time I found myself being favored. I heard the Pharaoh say, "I have set thee over all the land of Egypt." He placed a ring on my finger and a gold chain around my neck. I was now over all the land of Egypt and eventually was reunited with my family.

Joseph was a young man who had a dream of his family kneeling before him. It took several years for that dream to come to pass. I imagine there were several times when Joseph forgot about his dream and wondered where God was in all of this. He knew he had

God's favor, but did not understand everything going on in his life. Through the dark times, I believe God was growing Joseph up and leading him to a dependency upon Him. God had to take everything away from Joseph, stripping him of self, so the only thing he could rely upon was God and His power.

Do you feel at times you have been thrown in a pit or feel like you are in prison, asking, "God, where are you?" Maybe God is trying to do something in our lives and stripping us of our independence and teaching us how to depend on Him. God wants His creation to be dependent upon Him and trust in His power to work through us. We are designed to be with Him and rely upon His power to work a specific purpose in each one of us, for His glory.

The world teaches us to be independent, but God wants to train us to become dependent. God is in process of growing us up, and may have to take us through some valleys. We will never be able to pull off His purpose for our lives in our own power, and we cannot leverage His power for our purpose. Many of us feel the greatest problems are around us, but the greatest battles we face in life are within us. God designed us to be dependent on Him, and we tend to ask Him to change everything around us when He wants to change us from the inside. God won't further His purpose in our lives until we are ready.

Gary from Crossroads Atlanta quotes, "The first thing God wants to do is change you, not the things around you. God begins to form things in us and we become a trustworthy people and engage in community. You begin to win with others and love them as your neighbor. When we make God the center of our life, we will love ourselves, and we will know where our identity lies and will not fall victim to competing or comparing to anyone, and we will not have to accumulate stuff to be recognized as someone in this world. Our significance and identity is found in Christ, not in the patterns of this world."

So we must be prepared for anything God has for us, knowing God is with us and will never leave us. God is working His plan for our lives, but in those moments we must trust Him in what He is taking us through. We may feel like we are in personal hell, but understand God is doing a good work in us and will bring His plan for our life to pass for His glory. It may take years, but it is His desire to bless us and place a ring on our finger and put a gold chain around our necks.

Jesus,

Thank You for taking us through hard times. Thank You for never leaving us, and completing Your plan through us. I pray we would allow You to change us from the inside and form us into what You want us to become. I pray we would seek You first in everything we do, and never against ask where You are, but know You are in control.

"Greatest Day"

Romans 6:23

"For the wages of sin is death; but the gift of God is eternal life through Jesus Christ our Lord." – NIV

John 3:16

"For God so loved the world, that he gave his only begotten Son, that whosoever believeth in him should not perish, but have everlasting life." – NIV

I fell to my knees. The burden of sin was heavy upon me, my heart was empty, and I had lost my way. Tears filled my eyes and chills ran through my body like the flu. The pastor placed his hand on my shoulder and led me in the salvation prayer to receive Jesus Christ. Years of shame, grief, and rebellion poured from my soul the moment I had finished praying and accepting Jesus as my Lord and Savior. The empty hole in my heart was filled, the heavy burden of sin was lifted, and new tears of joy were shed.

I can honestly say it was the greatest day of my life! The presence of Jesus in me had changed my life in ways I really had not begun to understand. Why did I go home and immediately get rid of all my partying paraphernalia, stopped going to my local hangouts, and broke off relationships? I even recall a time when I went back to a bowling alley because I forgot to pay for my shoe rental. Could it be a changed heart, a heart cleansed and filled with everlasting love?

Let me ask you a question: What was the greatest day of your life? Some people may reply, "The birth of my son or daughter, the day I stepped foot on the moon, the day we won the World Series, the day I became a millionaire." If you have not experienced the gift of accepting Jesus into your heart, then you have not experienced the greatest day of your life yet. Jesus Christ desires to give new life to everyone who asks for it. Nothing in this world will ever compare to the gift Jesus has for you and me.

The greatest day in Jesus' life was dying on the cross. You may be wondering why, or be questioning why. His death on the cross was the only way we could have access to spend eternity with God. God loved us so much, He allowed His only Son to be crucified and buried. However, on the third day, Jesus arose from the grave and lives today. He wants to live in us, through us, and reach out to those who need a drink of living water. John 4:10: "Jesus answered and said unto her, If thou knewest the gift of God, and who it is that saith to thee, Give me to drink; thou wouldest have asked of him, and he would have given thee living water." - KJV

Jesus wants to give you the greatest day of your life … ask Him to become Lord of your life, and watch your life change before your very eyes.

Lord Jesus,

Thank You for sacrificing Your life so we could have eternal life. Thank You for Your grace and mercy You give us each day. I pray we would put You first and allow You to work in us and through us to accomplish Your plan. I pray for those who have not experienced the greatest day of their lives, which today would be that day!

"Grip of Grace"

Psalm 20:6

"Now I know that the LORD saves his anointed; he answers him from his Holy Heaven with the saving power of his right hand."
– NIV

Standing on the edge of the pool, gripped with fear at age three, I asked, "Are you sure you will watch me, Dad?" All the noise around the pool seemed to disappear as I focused on my father's clear and direct voice. "Trust me, Brian, go ahead, jump in and swim to me." My eyes were glued on my father, and my fears melted away.

Stepping out from the deck of the pool, I totally trusted my father to be there if I got in trouble. I hit the water with a splash and I began to thrash my arms and feet in all different directions. I took my eyes off my father for a minute, and I found myself struggling to keep afloat. I took in a gulp of water and panic immediately set in. I gasped for air crying, "Dad, Dad, help me!"

A strong arm gripped me and a powerful voice said, "Brian, stop, look at me, everything is okay!" My panic-filled eyes made contact with my father's eyes, and I knew everything was going to be okay as we waded to the edge of the pool.

This story reminded me of a disciple named Peter who stepped off a sinking boat to walk with Jesus on the water. He leaped out of the boat focused on Jesus, but allowed the effects of the wind and waves to steal his faith from him, resulting in a fearing man crying out to Jesus, "Lord, save me!" But the moment Peter refocused his eyes on Jesus, he was saved by the grip of grace.

If you feel like you are being pounded by the wind and waves, and gasping for life, there is a very simple solution to your problem. Take your eyes off the problem and put them back on Jesus. Our father is always with us, and walks with us through the storms of life. Notice I said "He walks with us through the storm." He will bring us out of the storm to safety. Keep your faith in Jesus, no matter what the problem is, because He is larger than anything we will face.

I like what Oral Roberts said, "God never asks you to do anything by yourself. You don't have to feel alone because God is closer to you than your breath." We can trust the Lord because he will never fail us. He will never fail you!

I wanted to close with a powerful poem from an unknown author.

> *I had walked life's way with easy tread,*
> *Had followed where comforts and pleasures led,*
> *Until one day in a quiet place,*
> *I met the Master face-to-face.*
>
> *I met him and knew him and blushed to see,*
> *That his eyes full of sorrow were fixed on me.*
> *And I faltered and fell at his feet that day,*
> *While my castles melted and vanished away.*
> *Melted and vanished and in their place,*
>
> *Naught else could see, but my Master's face.*
> *And I cried aloud, Oh!, make me meet*
> *To follow the steps of thy wounded feet.*
>
> *My thought is now for the souls of men.*
> *I've lost my life to find it again.*
> *E'er since that day in a quiet place,*
> *I met the Master face-to-face.*

Lord Jesus,

It is so easy for us to drown in our problems, and take our eyes off our source of strength. Forgive us, Lord, for trusting in anything but You. We thank You for Your grip of grace that brings us safely through.

"Heavy Load"

Matthew 11:28

"Come to Me, all you who labor and are heavy-laden and over-burdened, and I will cause you to rest. [I will ease and relieve and refresh your souls.]" - AMP

Face turning blue, pulse racing, I attempted to scream, "Help!" My attempt was futile. I had no more strength left in my arms, as the crushing weight pressed upon my chest. The pain was becoming unbearable, and in a second attempt, I reached deep within my lungs to grasp air and scream "Help, Mom!" Within seconds, my mother rushed to my room, to discover I had been pinned down by a couple hundred pounds of weight.

She exclaimed, "I can't pull this off you, Brian!" I asked her to start stripping off weight from one side of the bar I had been trying to bench press, thinking I would eventually be able to handle the load. As one side of the bar was stripped, the opposite side became uneven in weight distribution and gravity forced the bar to fly from my chest, into a nearby closet, with a loud crash that echoed throughout the house! The load was more than I could handle, and with no spotter to help me, it resulted in a situation I could not control. I was in trouble, and if my mother had not heard my cry for help, I do not know what would have happened to me, as I was totally exhausted when she came to my rescue.

Last night, I was reminded of the experience after looking at the way I have been living my life currently. I am at the point of exhaustion, trying to take on more than I can handle. Instead of taking things one day at a time, I have been trying to make things happen overnight, and it is crushing the air out of me. I learned something, and I believe it can help us strip unnecessary weight from our lives. If we allow our worries, anxieties, and problems to pin us down, eventually we will be tired and become crushed under the burden. Jesus can strip that from us if we will call on his name. According to His will, He can come to our rescue and give us rest.

Jesus died for all of us. He took all the crushing weight of the world's sins, and He carried them on his back to Mt. Calvary. All we have to do is take up our cross daily and walk with Him. What weight do you need to strip from your life? What is crushing the breath out of you? Jesus has given us a spotter named the Holy Spirit, who can make the heaviest loads seem light as a feather. We have to rely upon Jesus to get us through each day, and not allow the things of this world to weigh us down. Do not take on more than we can handle, as it will only put us into a sticky situation.

Lord Jesus,

Thank You for taking the heavy burden of our sins to the cross, and lifting them from us if we would accept You into our life. Thank You for giving us the Holy Spirit as our helper when the things we take on become too heavy for us to handle. I pray we would not allow worry, anxiety, and strife to weigh us down, and know where our strength lies in our weakness.

"I Love You This Much"

Jeremiah 31:3

"The Lord hath appeared of old unto me, saying, Yea, I have loved thee with an everlasting love: therefore with loving kindness have I drawn thee." – KJV

John 3:16

"For God so loved the world, that he gave his only begotten Son, that whosoever believeth in him should not perish, but have everlasting life." – KJV

Our eyes were glued on my father as he opened one of his presents from our mother. He was very meticulous about opening his package. His fingers carefully lifted under the seams of tape to separate the tape from the wrapping paper. He carefully removed the bow and ribbon without a tear. It was taking forever, and both my brother and I were becoming impatient as we anxiously waited to see what was hidden in the beautifully wrapped gift. Finally, he cracked open the box and reveled his gifts to us.

He removed the first gift from the box, which was a brand new watch. The second gift was some smelly aftershave, and the final gift was a simple statue to place on his desk at work. I picked up the statue and read the inscription on the base. It read "I LOVE YOU THIS MUCH!" The arms on the little women reached wide, signifying just how much love was being expressed, and a huge smile was painted on her face. I asked my mom, "How much do you love Dad?" She responded with a physical motion resembling the statue, with her arms stretched wide, and said, "This much and more!" I looked over towards my father and noticed a smile come across his face as tears filled his eyes.

Do you know you have someone who loves you more than anything in this world? Nothing can or will compare to the love that the Lord Jesus Christ has for you and me. He loved every one of us, and showed mankind how much by stretching His arms wide and taking nails in His hands and feet on a rugged wooden cross. Jesus dying at Calvary sent all of God's creation a message. Arms stretched wide, bruised and bleeding, Jesus was saying with His body, "I LOVE YOU THIS MUCH AND MORE!" With tears in his eyes and a peaceful smile across his face, He gave up His life for you and me.

Let me ask you a question: "How much do you love Jesus Christ?" When you look at Him stretched out on a cross, does it bring a smile to your face, knowing He bought your freedom, and does it bring tears of joy knowing he died to take away all your sins? He died on the cross for one reason, and that reason is YOU! Accept Him, and He will love you back with the greatest love you will ever experience.

Lord Jesus,

Thank You so much for expressing how much You love us my stretching your arms wide on a cross. Thank You for loving us so much and doing such an act to redeem us for eternity. I pray we would never forget the sacrifice You made, and I hope all of mankind would look to You with smiles on their faces and tears in their eyes.

"Invincible"

Psalm 54:15-17

"In righteousness shalt thou be established: thou shalt be far from oppression; for thou shalt not fear: and from terror; for it shall not come near thee. Behold, they shall surely gather together, but not by me: whosoever shall gather together against thee shall fall for thy sake. Behold, I have created the smith that bloweth the coals in the fire, and that bringeth forth an instrument for his work; and I have created the waster to destroy. No weapon that is formed against thee shall prosper; and every tongue that shall rise against thee in judgment thou shalt condemn." – KJV

Stepping boldly out of my cardboard spaceship with helmet in hand, I shouted at the top of my lungs towards my friends, "You can't kill me, your ray-guns will not be able to penetrate my super space armor, and you can't catch me because my thruster-boots are engaged!" As a child, my imagination always ran wild with inventions and ideas, leading to one concluding thought: You can't kill me because I am invincible!

Can you remember when you were shot several times by your friend, the opposing force, and you refused to die? In your mind, you were thinking of ways to stay alive, including making up some gadget that would surround you with an indestructible force field. You would make up excuses like, "I 'm not dead yet, your bomb only penetrated the outer shell of my invisible shield," or "You did not realize I had consumed my cell rejuvenation formula before stepping into battle."

Do you realize we are surrounded by the most powerful source in the universe? Through the blood of Jesus, we are promised protection. We can stand on the promises of God, because God does not lie. He loves us so much and does not want anything to happen to us. There are going to be times when it seems God is not there, and we may ask the question, "Why did this happen to me, Lord?"

The Lord's Word tells us that opposition will gather against us, but it is not of God. Negative actions, words, and thoughts allow the devil to get a foothold in our lives. The devil has one objective, and that is to destroy us any way he can. The Lord gives us words of strength, telling us we will not be oppressed, and not to fear terror because it will not come near us. His promise resembles my thinking as a child, when I boldly burst out of my spaceship knowing nothing could hurt me.

God created the destroyer, the devil. The devil was an angelic being before he fell from Heaven, taking a third of the angels with him. Every weapon the devil tries to use against us will not prosper. The power of the Holy Spirit resides in us, and we can cast down anything the devil throws at us through the name of Jesus Christ. And any tongue that rises up against us, we shall condemn in the name of Jesus. If you read verse seventeen in Psalm 54 closely, you will see God giving us power through the Holy Spirit to condemn anything that stands against us. The only way we can be defeated is by allowing the devil to penetrate our minds with his lies.

We can boldly step out in life daily, and know in our minds we are protected with supernatural armor and through the name of Jesus we are invincible against our enemy, the devil. I like what Jessie Duplantis quoted in one of his monthly newsletters: "Each time I want to look at the devil, all I have to do is lift up my shoe." The good news is that we do not have to invent or think up any gadgets for protection. All we have to do is stand on the promises God made to us through His Word, and believe in the strength of the Lord.

The next time you feel wounded or defeated by the devil, open your Bible to Psalm 54 and read, then stand up and claim that you are invincible through the name of Jesus. Do not give in to the devil and his lies. Shout from the top of your lungs, "I am not defeated by you, devil, your weapons can do nothing to me because of what God promised me! You have no control over my mind or life, and I bind you and command you to take your hands off me, in the Name of Jesus!" The devil will leave because he has to, but he will be back for another battle, waiting for you to emerge from life unprotected.

Lord Jesus,

Thank You for the promises we have in Your Word. Thank You for shedding Your blood on the cross for us and giving us Your living Word to live by. I pray that we would be encouraged daily in Your Word, and know in our minds we have power over the devil and no weapon he forms against us will prosper. One drop of Your blood shields us and brings to pass all God's promises for us.

"Living or Dying"

John 15:5

" I am the vine; you are the branches. If a man remains in me and I in him, he will bear much fruit; apart from me you can do nothing. If anyone does not remain in me, he is like a branch that is thrown away and withers; such branches are picked up, thrown into the fire and burned." – NIV

Glistening from fresh drops from the previous night's rain, the roses displayed their beauty in the early morning sunlight. Some of the rose bush's stems where healthy and strong, thriving with new life. I noticed a few of the vines were lifeless. During a transplant, some of the roots supplying life to those branches were accidentally damaged. The dead vines were dark and dry compared to the other flourishing vines, and below the dried dead vines lay their decaying debris.

Last year, I decided to transplant a rose bush to a new area of my yard. I tried to be as careful as possible in the process of digging it up, but some of the main roots to the vines were severed in the process. At first I thought the rose bush would not be salvageable, however, I decided to proceed with the transplant and created the perfect atmosphere for the rose bush, and hoped for the best.

Early last spring, the rose bush started to display some life when rosebuds began to appear. Half of the rose bush showed positive signs from the transplant, but the other half did not. The two main vines were connected, one was living and the other was dead. Some of the healthy vines were intertwined with the dead ones, and the once fully alive, fruitful rose bush had been scarred forever. I wound up cutting the dead vines from the rose bush and tossing them in the trash.

Jesus wants to be rooted deeply with us, so He can nourish us with the Holy Spirit, and give us life. If our roots have been severed from Him, we will not bear fruit and surely die. Are we rooted with Christ? Do our actions, words, and thoughts bear fruit for the glory of God? We can do nothing without the Lord, and we have the power through Jesus Christ to do everything according to His will. We can be those beautiful roses, or we can be useless, thorn-less, lifeless vines. The choice is ours. However, we need to remember Jesus is always ready to give us life and He can restore life to those who feel dead and useless.

Lord Jesus,

Thank You for the love that passes all understanding, and for Your desire to give life to those who call upon Your name. I pray we would desire to remain in the vine that brings life and produces fruit, rather than severing ourselves from the vine that gives life, only to suffer from a fruitless life.

"Naughty or Nice"

Ecclesiastes 12:14

"For God will bring every work into judgment, with every secret thing, whether it be good, or whether it be evil." - KJV

1 John 1:9

"If we confess our sins, he is faithful and just to forgive us our sins, and to cleanse us from all unrighteousness." – KJV

W e stood with our parents in line for hours, waiting to see Santa Claus. The line stretched halfway around the mall lobby, and every few minutes my brother and I would lean out of line, checking to make sure Santa and his helper were still there. Our eyes locked onto Santa like a missile locked on its target. We slowly made our way toward the front of the line. Finally, as we approached Santa, uneasiness came over me.

"Ho…Ho…Ho…" belted from Santa as he looked down from his chair at my brother and me. He said, "Have you boys been naughty or nice this year?" I think my reply took the life right out of my parents when I replied, "Naughty, Santa!" My brother just remained silent and his eyes spoke volumes with a crazy look of disbelief. I think Santa was surprised, too, when I told him I was expecting a lump of coal this year. Santa quickly corrected me and said, "I appreciate your honesty, but you have done more nice things, and I have you on my nice list this year."

Earlier that week, my mother told me if I kept being bad, I would find a lump of coal in my stocking from Santa. Well, I took that to heart and was convinced my behavior ruined Christmas. I can remember being very sad, thinking there would be nothing under the tree this year with my name on it, and hanging from our fireplace would be my stocking filled with a large lump of coal. What a nightmare! I never realized how serious Santa Claus was on the subject until after watching a Christmas show called, *Santa Claus is Coming to Town.*

Do you realize every one of us deserves a stocking full of coal because we have all been naughty in the eyes of God? But there is one who saved Christmas for us all with a gift of His mercy and grace. All we have to do is accept this gift, and immediately every-thing you and I did naughty will be wiped clean from the list, and our names can be recorded on the nice list for eternity.

Jesus Christ came to the earth, ministered God's love, and died a sacrificial death on the cross, taking on the sins of the world. Salvation is a free gift to anyone who wants to receive, and everyone is qualified no matter what we have done. We can start over with a new life in Christ and forget anything we have done wrong in the past, because God will forget it all and never bring it up again. So, make sure your name is on the nice list for eternity and rid yourself of the stocking of coal once and for all.

Lord Jesus,

Thank You for giving us the greatest present of all time, Your love, mercy, and grace. By accepting Jesus, we can rid ourselves of everything we have done not pleasing to God, and by continu-ally confessing things to Jesus, all our wrongs will be cast away forever. I pray we would seriously take a look at our lives and ask ourselves the question: "Have I been naughty or nice?" If we have been naughty, we need to accept the gift that will take it all away. If we have been nice, we need to continue to examine our thoughts, actions, and words, bringing them into the glory of the Lord.

"No Fear"

Isaiah 41:10

" Fear thou not; for I am with thee: be not dismayed; for I am thy God: I will strengthen thee; yea, I will help thee; yea, I will uphold thee with the right hand of my righteousness." – KJV

Eyes the size of golf balls, sweat dripping from my brow, I edged my way toward the exit. Feeling like a cow in a slaughter line, the fear of death raced in my mind. I peered over the shoulder of the man in front of me, and noticed the line getting shorter and shorter. Soon it would be my turn, and I frantically began checking my equipment to make sure everything was ready. Everything I learned over the past eight weeks scrambled in my mind, forcing me to panic. I thought, "This is not worth it, and I would really like to get off now!" But it was too late, and I found myself handing my static line to the jumpmaster, hearing the command "Go" as I exited the C-141 aircraft.

"One thousand one, one thousand two, one thousand three," I was thinking as I fell through the air. Eyes tightly shut, fearing the worst, I placed my hand on the reserve parachute's ripcord. My heart was now beating out of control, and all the training videos of jumps gone badly grasped a foothold on my mind. I had to be nuts to place all my trust in the person who packed the chute strapped to my back. The fall seemed endless, and my fear grew stronger. My hand was cemented to the emergency ripcord, and I was prepared to pull it. However, I felt the static line pull me like a rag in the wind. The line released, pulling the air chute from my pack, and my parachute followed, with a loud pop filling with air. Everything was now silent, and I opened my eyes to discover my chute had fully deployed.

The fear was quickly replaced with peace and joy, and I was able to enjoy my descent from a few thousand feet. The view was incredible, and my line of sight seemed endless. There was nothing wrong with the equipment issued to me, however, my mind had convinced me otherwise before the jump. One moment, I was thinking I would be falling to my death, and moments later, I had no fear once I saw my equipment was fully operational. In Psalm 18-22, you will see that our life is ultimately in God's hands. The NIV Promise Keepers Bible says it best: "Our modern society surrounds us with cushions and protections that range from seat belts to dead bolts, from warning labels to health insurance. Wisdom tells us to use these things to protect ourselves. But ultimately and finally, the psalmist reminds us, 'We wait in hope for the Lord'; he is our help and our shield." (v. 20).

Regardless of what other protections we have, our only sense of security must be in Jesus Christ. The size of our God is the size of our security and peace. What do you fear? The only thing we should fear is God. He is the one who has packed all our parachutes of life, and ultimately our lives are in his hands. Psalms 34:7 says, "The angel of the Lord encamps around those who fear Him, and He delivers them." We can stop clinging to the emergency ripcord of fear and open our eyes, because we have security in Jesus Christ. Do not allow the devil to get a foothold on your mind and tell you otherwise. Remember, in the name of Jesus we can move mountains and do all things according to His will.

So we can confidently step up to the open door of life and jump out, knowing our equipment is fully operational because it was packed by God. We can take those jumps in life, knowing that Jesus Christ is jumping right by our side and he is there to guide us and direct us safely to the ground.

Lord Jesus,

Thank You for caring so much about us and loving us beyond anything we can imagine. Thank You for promising to be with us and never to leave us nor forsake us, once we place our lives in Your hands. I pray we would break the grip of fear on our lives and boldly jump into life, knowing we do not have to fear, because we know You are with us on every jump we make.

"One Cry Away"

Revelation 3:20

"Behold, I stand at the door, and knock: if any man hear my voice, and open the door, I will come in to him, and will sup with him, and he with me." - KJV

Psalm 34:15

"The eyes of the LORD are upon the righteous, and his ears are open unto their cry." -KJV

It was amazing to watch what two parents would go through for their offspring. Traveling thousands of miles, nearly starving to death, they would protect and raise one baby per season. The survival rate of the newborn totally relied upon the diligence of the parents. If the parents failed in any part of the process, the baby and parents could die.

I am talking about a movie called *The March of the Penguins.* The parents would travel thousands of miles from the ocean to have a hatching, a process very long and tedious. In summary, both parents would march for days, mate, and wait several months for one baby to hatch. To survive, each parent had to take turns traveling back to the ocean to feed and return to nourish one another.

The mother would hatch the egg and pass it to the father before she traveled back to the ocean, and the father protected the egg by placing it on top of his feet and sheltering it with his body for months during severe weather conditions. After the baby penguin hatched, the father would regurgitate food stored in his belly to nourish the chick, as they both continue to wait for the mother to return with fresh food. Upon the arrival of the mother, the father and new chick would greet her with open mouths and empty bellies. Then the father would memorize the sound of the baby's voice so he could find them, after returning from his long journey from the ocean to nourish the mother and baby. If one of the parents were killed in the process, the baby and surviving parent would eventually die from starvation.

You are probably wondering, "Your point, Brian, is?" Well, here it is. After several months, the father returns to a flock of thousands and thousands of screaming babies protected by their mothers. He stands away from the pack, rolls his head like radar, listening for that one still voice of the baby penguin he memorized. To me, all the cries sounded the same on film, yet the father picked out his baby's voice amongst thousands of other babies crying in the artic air, and was united with his mate and baby forever. The important thing to remember is if the father did not know his baby's voice prior to leaving on his journey to the sea for food, then upon his return, he would have been unsuccessful in his reunion and they would have been separated, leading to the death of the mate and baby.

The Lord Jesus Christ knows our voices, but we have to cry out to Him to be connected to the Father forever in eternity. If we do not cry out to accept Jesus Christ as our Savior and Lord, then we will be separated from the Father forever and die in our sin. The Lord knows every one of us by name, knows the number of hairs on our heads, and created us before we were ever conceived by our parents. The Lord is patiently waiting for all His children to call His name, so He can find them and reside with them forever. If we fail to link up with the Father, we will be alienated from our creator and will not receive the gift of eternal life.

Please do not put your decision off another day. We may not be here tomorrow, so secure your future eternally with God through Jesus Christ. He is standing close by, listening for your cry to Him. Call on the name of Jesus, believe He died for your sins, and believe He was raised from the dead to live in your heart today. He wants to be united with you forever, and does not wish to see you standing in the cold all alone, separated from your Creator.

Lord Jesus,

Thank You for bridging the gap so we can be with the Father forever. Thank You for knowing everything about us to include our name. I pray for all of creation to not wait another day, and call on the name of Jesus to be united with God forever in eternity. I pray none would be left behind to freeze in the cold.

"Pinned In a Corner?"

Ephesians 6:10

"Finally, my brethren, be strong in the Lord, and in the power of his might." – NIV

The announcements and introductions were made as both fighters stood toe-to-toe. Their stares at each other could melt steel. They touched gloves and retreated to neutral corners, anticipating the bell. *Ding!* The bell sounded, echoing throughout the arena, and both fighters rushed to the center of the ring. The fighters were on their toes, circling each other. As one threw a quick jab, the opposite fighter would quickly counter with a double jab and overhand right. The adrenaline built as they sized up each other for battle. Numerous jabs were thrown in the first round, but both fighters were cautious about attacking each other with full force.

Ding! The bell rang … round two. The fighter in the red trunks rushed toward his opponent, unleashing a flurry of punches. He backed his opponent in the corner and hit him with a series of hooks, upper cuts, overhands, and body blows. The fighter in the white trunks tried to gain his composure, blocking some of the stinging punches. He waited for the perfect time to counter with an upper cut to the jaw of his opponent in red. You could hear the impact from across the arena as the fighter in red was thrown back from the force of the crushing punch. The fighter in white quickly moved in for the kill, and was victorious in landing a series of blows, knocking him out and winning the fight in the second round.

All it took was one punch. Something in a fighter's heart was not going to allow his opponent to beat him. At times, it takes being thrown in a corner and being bombarded with punches to bring out the hidden warrior in a fighter. It is so easy to lose heart and give up when we are under pressure from the blows in life. Some of us are afraid to get into the ring and fight, due to hidden fears. It is so easy to become fearful and lose confidence in ourselves, forgetting who we really are in Christ.

There is someone in us who will never give up on us, no matter what. His name is Jesus, and He will give us strength to counter those stinging punches. The devil wants to keep us trapped in a corner, driving fear in us, convincing us we do not have what it takes to win. We need to wait for the perfect timing of God, and counter the devil with an upper cut blow, knocking him back, and then use the Word of God to knock him out!

Do not allow the devil to beat you. Tighten the strings on your gloves, bite down on your mouthpiece, and jump into the ring to fight with everything you've got! Do not give up. Trust in the Lord's strength to get you through.

Lord Jesus,

Thank You for promising never to leave us nor forsake us. Thanks for being our strength in our weakness. I pray we would have no fear to stand toe-to-toe with our opposing force, the devil, and have confidence our victory is in You alone. I pray we would find strength in you each time we face the heavy blows of life.

"Point of Weakness"

Ephesians 6:10-12

"Finally, my brethren, be strong in the Lord, and in the power of his might. Put on the whole armor of God, that ye may be able to stand against the wiles of the devil. For we wrestle not against flesh and blood, but against principalities, against powers, against the rulers of the darkness of this world, against spiritual wickedness in high places." – KJV

My brother and I had been taking Judo lessons for a few months, and our instructor informed us our first official competition was to take place that coming weekend. Would all the training pay off? What if I forget something? Will it lead to my defeat? These were a few questions I asked myself on our journey home from practice.

The big day finally arrived; our team arrived to the competition early, making final preparations for the matches. We weighed in and placed our names on one side of the match board, identifying who we would fight. I cinched my yellow belt tightly around my waist as we waited for our rivals to emerge from the locker room.

They walked in and sat across from us after placing their names on the board. You could feel the adrenaline flowing and the egos begin to flare. Everyone looked confident, strong, and victorious. There was no hiding of strength or weakness in the sport, and soon we would face off with our opponents. One would walk away victorious and the other in defeat. I was defeated by my opponent because he discovered a point of weakness and took advantage of it, leading him to victory in the match.

The Lord gives us His armor for a reason. The armor of God is designed to protect our weak points. The devil knows our weakness and will attack those specific areas. If we allow the enemy to get a foothold on our lives, it becomes harder to defend ourselves. Paul is telling us not to take this lightly, as it is the devil's objective to destroy our walks with the Lord, forcing us to sin against God.

In Ephesians 6:13-18, Paul describes all seven pieces of the armor we must wear to be victorious in battle. All these are very important in protection from our enemy, the devil. Upon awakening, we need to put on the armor of God so we can be prepared versus being unprepared, exposing our weakness. I have discovered it can be very difficult to put on the armor of God while in the middle of a battle.

Let's be prepared, so the next time we are facing our opponent the devil in battle, he will quickly discover God's strength in us and flee. Take time each morning and ask the Lord to arm you in his armor. Name each piece as you place it on your body.

Paul's expert advice to us: "Wherefore take unto you the whole armor of God, that ye may be able to withstand in the evil day, and having done all, to stand. Stand therefore having

1) your loins girt with truth, **(Belt)**
2) and having on the breastplate of righteousness; **(Breastplate)**
3) And your feet shod with the preparation of the gospel of peace; **(Sandals)**
4) Above all, taking the shield of faith, wherewith ye shall be able to quench all the fiery darts of the wicked. **(Shield)**
5) And take the helmet of salvation, **(Helmet)**
6) And the sword of the Spirit, which is the word of God: **(Sword)**
7) Praying always with all prayer and supplication in the Spirit.... **(God's Word)**

Lord Jesus,

Thank You we can live in Your strength and not rely upon our own. Thank You for giving us Your armor, knowing what battles we will face while here on earth. I pray all my brothers and sisters in Christ would make it a habit each day to put on the seven pieces of armor, trusting You with their lives.

"Press Forward"

Philippians 3:14

"I press toward the mark for the prize of the high calling of God in Christ Jesus." – NIV

I heard "Steenhoek, front and center!" blare from the commander's mouth. Snapping to attention, I ran to the front of the company formation, saluted, and replied, "Yes, Sir." The command was issued. I would carry the company colors in the morning battalion run. I would be running between the company commander and the first sergeant. There was no backing out from the order, and the whole company counted on me to wave our colors with pride as we passed other companies in the 82nd Airborne.

"C-130 sitting on the strip, paratroopers going to take a little trip, stand up, hookup, shuffle to the door, out the door and count to four, one! two! three! four!; if my chute doesn't open wide, tell my mother not to cry." This was one of the cadences we used during the six mile run.

Looking to my right then to my left, I adjusted my pace to stay in step with the commander and first sergeant. We approached the three mile mark and my arms were beginning to burn from the weight of the company flag. I found myself falling a couple paces behind the commander, and immediately picked up the pace to regain balance in the ranks. The weight of the flag was beginning to take a toll on me and I had to make an extra effort to hide my weakness from the commander.

The burning in my arms intensified and the colors began to droop from their original forty-five degree position. Everything in my body was telling me to give in and surrender. "Steenhoek, everything in order soldier?" came from the first sergeant as he glanced over at me. In my semi-exhausted voice, I replied, "Yes, first sergeant!" But I was thinking: *How am I going to get to the finish line?*

One mile left, passing another Special Forces company, I held high the colors of the First Seventeenth Calvary. My arms felt like they were going to fall off as I mustered all the strength I had left to maintain the height of our colors until the company completely passed us. The length of the company seemed to go forever, like a train never ending. Finally the last rank of soldiers passed like a caboose of the train and the run was almost over. I made it with company colors in hand!

At times, we feel like giving up from the burning pressures of life. The weight seems unbearable and slows our pace. The Apostle Paul told us we need to press forward to the finish line. When we feel like giving up, remember who we are running with in the ranks. God, Jesus, and the Holy Spirit are right by our side and will sustain us through the battalion run. The next time you feel like surrendering, look to your right and left, gain strength from the Lord, hold your head high and do not give up!

Lord Jesus,

Thank You for running with us in the busyness of this world. Thank you for strengthening us when we fall behind. I pray we would set a goal to press forward toward the prize and give You all the glory and honor.

"Reach Out and Touch Him"

Luke 8:43-46

"And a woman having an issue of blood twelve years, which had spent all her living upon physicians, neither could be healed of any, came behind Him, and touched the border of His garment: and immediately her issue of blood stanched. And Jesus said, 'Who touched me?' When all denied, Peter and they that were with Him said, 'Master, the multitude throng thee and press thee, and sayest thou, who touched me?' And Jesus said, 'Somebody hath touched me: for I perceive that virtue is gone out of me.'" – KJV

W hat faith this woman had in Christ Jesus. I wish I had faith like that at times in my walk with the Lord. This woman had been suffering for many years with a blood disorder, and everyone she sought for help told her it was hopeless. She spent all her living on trying to become well, and no one was able to help her.

You may be facing one of those times in your life today. It seems like there is no light at the end of the tunnel, and everyone has told you it is hopeless. I feel the Lord has given me this message to strengthen you and tell you, "DO NOT GIVE UP!" There is an answer to your problem.

You may be facing something life-threatening, or you are faced with something very overwhelming. I do not know what the issue is, but my heart is burdened to get this message to you. The answer I have for you is simple and his name is Jesus. He is waiting for you to reach out and touch Him.

Just look what happened to the lady who was hopeless, after touching the outer garment of her Savior. She was immediately healed of her condition. How did she receive immediate healing? By having strong FAITH in Jesus. I imagine what this lady felt each time her hopes were dashed after hearing the reports of doctors. I can see in my mind the look on her face after she caught a glimpse of the Savior walking through the crowd.

Weak from this blood disorder, she had to push through a mob of people to get to Jesus. She had to crawl, and I bet she was trampled underfoot in pursuing her last hope. I can visualize this desperate pursuit, and see her reaching out with all her strength, touching Jesus as He walked by. She did not believe what the world was telling her. She placed her faith in God, and did not let doubt stop her from getting healing from the one source she knew could heal her through one touch.

Jesus is waiting for us to reach out and touch Him in faith. He wants to bring blessing and healing into our lives. We have to push through everything that hinders us, and take doubt from our minds. We may feel trampled at times, but do not give up on Jesus. Reach out to one who can restore, as He is the same today as He was that day, walking through the crowd. He wants to say to you, "Who touched me?"

Do not believe anything other than God's Word. Stand on the Word of God and expect His promises to come to pass in your life. Let your faith lead you to the Savior and reach out and touch Him today! He wants to be everything to you.

Lord Jesus,

Thank You for being there when we need you, and promising You would never leave us nor forsake us. Thank You that you are in the same business of blessing and healing today, as You were when You walked on this earth. I pray we would only listen to what Your Word says and learn to stand on your promises. I pray we would always walk with our arms extended, touching Your garment, and have faith You can do all things according to Your will.

"Roots of Life"

Jeremiah 17:8

"For he shall be as a tree planted by the waters, and that spreadeth out her roots by the river, and shall not see when heat cometh, but her leaf shall be green; and shall not be careful in the year of drought, neither shall cease from yielding fruit." – KJV

Sitting in the prayer garden, focusing on God, my attention was drawn toward an old tree standing a few yards from the bench I was seated on. The tree looked malnourished, lacking water, as some of the branches were dry and lifeless. Parts of the tree were still alive, as those branches swayed with life in the breeze. At the base of the tree, large limbs had been removed, and I watched sap bleed from the tree's scars.

The Lord then drew my attention to another tree in the prayer garden a few yards away. This tree was solid and full of life as it towered toward the sky. The branches looked strong and sturdy and the trunk was firmly rooted in the ground. It seemed to be the largest tree in the garden, and I could not help but notice all the life in its branches.

Finally, the Lord drew my attention to a frail, weak, baby tree, freshly planted in the radius of the last tree. Lines were tied to its branches, connected to stakes buried in the ground for stability. Buds were just beginning to bloom on the naked branches, as no real foliage had developed yet. I noticed the little tree being shadowed by the large tree and really paid no attention to it until God revealed the truth to me.

The old tree was a representation of my life before I found Jesus Christ. I was part dead, part alive, malnourished and polluted by the world. Scars were left from what people did or said to me, and I was bleeding un-forgiveness and bitterness.

Jesus was the second tree, full of strength and power. He is fully alive and His branches are full of life. Nothing can tip Him over, as His roots reach deep down in God's Word. His strength is made perfect in our weakness.

Can you guess what the little tree represented? Yes, me again, after accepting Christ, a new baby Christian released into the world. Lines from God, Jesus, and the Holy Spirit were tied to my branches as I begin to take root in Christianity. Buds from God's promises were beginning to bloom, and the shadow of Jesus was now my protection from the harsh elements of the world.

God told me to firmly plant my trunk in the ground and wrap my roots around the roots of Jesus Christ, and receive nourishment and life from His living water.

If you feel like the first tree, barely clinging to life, scared and abandoned, there is hope. Jesus wants to give us the roots of life, and all we have to do is accept His gift by faith. Jesus hung on a tree, the cross towering over the sins of the world. His blood was shed, dripping from the cross, soaking the earth, giving eternal life to all who believed He died at Calvary for their sins.

Jesus lives today. He rose from the dead and is the biggest, strongest, most powerful tree in the garden. He wants to give you living water, and is telling us to plant ourselves deep in His roots. We need to trust in His strength and allow His shadow to protect us from the evils of the world. We need to tap into the true source of power and allow His Word to flow in the veins of our branches, producing fruit for the Kingdom of God.

Lord Jesus,

Thank You for dying on the cross giving new life to all who believe You died for their sins. Thank You for rising from the dead, being the largest tree in the garden, and being a power source we can tap into to receive living water. I pray we would take our trunks and plant them deep in God's Word, wrapping around Your roots for life everlasting.

"Rotten Spot"

Isaiah 5:24

"Therefore as the fire devoureth the stubble, and the flame consumeth the chaff, so their root shall be as rottenness, and their blossom shall go up as dust: because they cast away the law of the Lord of hosts, and despised the word of the Holy one of Israel." – KJV

Returning from the local farmer's market, I reached down in the brown bag and retrieved a beautiful Washington Red Apple. I washed and rinsed the apple, being very careful not to bruise the outer skin. Beads of water glistening on the skin ran off like rain on a freshly waxed car. *Crunch.* As I took the first bite, I could feel the solid piece break off into my waiting mouth. The apple was healthy, fresh, and juicy.

The phone rang. Not wanting to be rude by eating in someone's ear, I placed the apple on the counter. The phone conversation lasted longer than expected, and I had forgotten about my apple. After hanging up the phone, it dawned on me where I had left my snack. Immediately, I picked up the apple and took a bite, to quickly discover the apple's consistency had changed. The once beautiful, healthy, juicy apple was rotten in the spot I had bitten into, after being exposed to the elements, and had to be cut out.

I cut out the exposed spot, and the rest of the apple, protected by its skin, delivered a juicy, fulfilling treat. The Lord immediately asked me in my Spirit, "Brian, do you have any rotten spots that need to be cut out?" We as Christians look like beautiful apples, full of life, healthy, and shiny. Once we expose ourselves to the elements of sin, the consistency of our Spirit changes. If sin is not removed immediately, the whole body will be affected. The skin of the apple hides all the defects and bruises not seen by the eye. We tend to hide our sin, hoping it would just disappear, but if not confessed, it can destroy a once beautiful, healthy, juicy apple.

The good news is, we have a thing called mercy and grace. Jesus is ready to cut out any rotten spots you may have and toss them down the garbage disposal. Jesus knows we are not perfect apples, and we expose ourselves to elements that destroy us. If we would confess our sin to Jesus, He is the only one who can restore us and bring healing to a rotten apple. We could be rotten to the core, yet He still loves us and wants to be in our lives. He will give us the protection we need from the harsh elements of sin, and it only takes one drop of his blood to wash us clean.

Lord Jesus,

Thank You for loving us, no matter what we did or who we may have hurt. Thank you that our sin can be removed by simply asking You to cut it out and throw it away. I pray we would be very careful with our skin and not allow decay to enter in. I pray we would be honest with ourselves and get rid of everything that is rotting our core.

"Seeing With Your Own Eyes"

Matthew 4:23

"And Jesus went about all Galilee, teaching in their synagogues, and preaching the gospel of the kingdom, and healing all manner of sickness and all manner of disease among the people." - KJV

W hen I was old enough, my parents gave me some news that would affect me for the rest of my life. At a young age, I realized my difference from everyone else around me, but thought it might only be temporary. I would hear children around me discuss simple things like the overwhelming beauty of the nature that lay before them. None of those things were real to me, because only darkness filled my world. My parents explained to me that I was blind from birth, and would be blind until the day I died. My life would be very challenging, and I could only imagine what everything looked like in this world that lay before me.

Can you imagine being blind from birth? I can recall an experiment I did in high school that portrayed the life of the blind. The teacher explained, "Imagine not seeing anything from birth, growing up blind, and trying to adapt with no sight. We can all see, so in our minds we picture what lays before us, but someone who is blind from birth has to be taught how things are shaped, colored, and designed." We were instructed to wear a blindfold for half the day, and rely on fellow students to help us get around. Stepping from light to darkness was a terrifying experience, and it was very difficult trusting others to help me. Especially after being led on a wild goose chase, having walked into a classroom in session, walking circles around the flagpole, and bumping into girls walking in the halls between classes.

This man mentioned in the Bible had never seen any light pass before his eyes, and only wondered what it would be like to see. He had been an outcast for all his life, and labeled a sinner by the people because of his blindness. All he could do was sit and beg every day, hoping his life would change for the better. Why was this man born blind? In John 9:3, we find the answer. "Neither this man nor his parents sinned," said Jesus, "but this happened so that the work of God might be displayed in his life." The light of life now stood before the man who could not see. He heard only the words from the lips of the stranger. "While I am in the world, I am the light of the world." Then he touched his eyes with tenderness, and moist mud covered his eyes. "Go wash in the pool of Siloam," Jesus instructed him.

In darkness, the man rushed to the pool to wash the mud from his eyes, and noticed beams of light rushing into his mind. He had never experienced or felt anything like it, and he took several blinks, allowing light to slowly come in. Overpowered by the light, he quickly closed his eyes to regain the security he had in darkness. I could only imagine how scared he was to allow light into his life, but once he did, the darkness would be gone forever. I could see the man opening his eyes very slowly, terrified and excited at the same time to discover the new world that lay before him. What would you do if you were blind all your life and now all a sudden could see everything? This man could only imagine what things looked like after being told by someone, but now he could see with his own eyes.

The light that penetrates darkness is Jesus, and the man could not only physically see, but also saw a different light that changed his life forever. If you read John chapter nine, you will see what this man did in the name of Jesus, and note he had never seen or believed in Jesus. He stood up to the Pharisees and shared his personal testimony of how Jesus healed him. He claimed, "This man is a prophet." His parents would not stand up for want Jesus did for their son, as they feared being thrown out of the synagogue. The once-blind man faced the Pharisees a second time, hearing the leaders say, "The man who healed you is a sinner and not from God." The now-seeing man replied, "Whether he is a sinner or not, I don't know. One thing I do know. I was blind, but now I see."

I want you to realize something in this story. The man who now could see stood bold for Jesus, who healed him. He had never laid eyes on Jesus, only heard his name, nor believed in Him before, but after what Jesus did, his whole outlook on life changed. His testimony was powerful, and it swayed many to believe in Jesus, including himself. In John 9:35, Jesus heard that they had thrown him out, and when he found him, he said, "Do you believe in the Son of Man?" "Who is he, sir?" the man asked. "Tell me so that I may believe in him." That day, that man not only could physically see, but the light of the world took away his spiritual blindness as well.

Jesus said, "For judgment I have come into this world, so that the blind will see and those who see will become blind." Do you realize, we are all spiritually blind at birth, and will grow in that blindness our entire life unless we allow the light of Jesus to shine in our eyes? Spiritual blindness only allows us to walk down the dark dead ends of this world. This blindness will lead us straight to death's door, if we do not decide to do something about it today. The things of this world will only build scales over our eyes, making it more difficult for the light to come in. As we become more accustomed to the darkness, we find peace and tranquility in darkness. Just what the devil wants.

Jesus said, "As long as it is day, we must do the work of Him who sent me. Night is coming, when no one can work." Jesus teaches us we can do nothing in the dark, and can only serve Him during the day. Jesus is the light that can heal us from our blindness, and He stands before us, waiting to hear us say, "Who is He sir? Tell me so that I may believe in Him." Jesus wants to touch our lives, take the scales from our eyes, and allow His love to fill our lives. All we have to do is allow Him to touch our lives by asking Him to take the darkness away and give us His light. Are you walking in darkness, and find yourself making circles in the dark, bumping into walls, or walking down dead ends? Ask Jesus to show you the light today, and begin seeing in a whole new way. Then stand bold for Jesus, and share your personal testimony to the world!

Lord Jesus,

We know You are the great physician, and through your stripes we have the gift of healing. Thank you for sacrificing Yourself at Calvary so we can have the power of light to overcome darkness. Without You, we are walking in darkness, but in You we have an everlasting light. My prayer is we would stay away from the darkness, which only brings confusion, strife, and fear, and cling to the light, which only brings peace and joy.

"Self- or God-Centered"

Luke 11:23

"He that is not with me is against me: and he that gathereth not with me scattereth." – KJV

The sheep are peacefully grazing in the pasture as the Shepherd keeps his eye on their every move. He knows the precise count of his flock, and can spot when one is weak, sick, or dying. In times of peril, he will gather all his sheep and protect them from the nearby threat, and even risk his own life to save one from the jaws of death. Not one of the flock can be lost, or the Shepherd would be held accountable. He desires all his sheep to lie down in peace, graze in rich pastures, and know they are well protected by their master.

Woe to the Shepherds of Israel who only take care of themselves! Should not Shepherds take care of their flocks? These are words of Ezekiel. He is rebuking the leaders of the Israelites, trying to instruct them to look out for the people and not themselves. Ezekiel said, "You eat the curds, clothe yourselves with wool and slaughter the choice animals, but do not take care of the flock." The leaders cared more about themselves, and less of those around them. Ruling over the people with unkindness and cruelty, forcing them to scatter and become food for the devil, they failed to strengthen the weak, heal the sick, or seek the lost.

What does God's Word teach us about this? "Because my Shepherds did not search for my flock but cared for themselves rather than for my flock, I am against the Shepherds and will hold them accountable for my flock." God hates when we place ourselves before others, knowing we were created to serve God and mankind. Are we self-centered or God-centered? Christians have a very important decision to make, and we will one day be held responsible for that decision. Do we want to be seen by God as a people who only cared for their own well being, or do we honor God by strengthening the weak, helping the sick, and searching for the lost?

God is calling us to action! There are millions of souls that have been scattered and destined for an eternity away from God. He does not desire to see one of his children separated from His loving hands. He wants to bring us all to a land filled with milk and honey, give us his best, and bring us into the fold of eternal life with Him forever. God tells us in his Word, "I Myself will search for my sheep and look after them. As a Shepherd looks after his scattered flock when he is with them, so will I look after my sheep, I will rescue them from all the places where they were scattered on a day of clouds and darkness."

One day we will all be held accountable for our actions, and will stand before Jesus in judgment. He will know if we have been faithful with the gift or gifts God has blessed us with. Did we glorify God, or did we abuse the gift and think only about ourselves? Spiritual gifts revolve around serving God and mankind. Paul tells us in 1 Corinthians 14:12 "So it is with you. Since you are eager to have Spiritual gifts, try to excel in gifts that build up the Church." The Church is Jesus Christ, and we are the body of the Church. Jesus is our Shepherd and we need to view Him as our role model. If one sheep is lost, we must leave the others, search for the one who is lost, and bring it back to the fold.

It is very hard to bear a resemblance to Jesus when we are only concerned about ourselves. The world labels it to be a good thing, condoning power, prestige, and self-centeredness. Jesus wants us to show His love, grace, and mercy to others so they may find truth in the darkness of sin. Do our actions, thoughts, and words reflect the character of a good Shepherd, or do they mirror a Shepherd only thinking about himself? Do we seek to build up the weak, help the sick, and search for the lost? I personally need to rethink my priorities in life, and it has been hard for me to put others first, but it can be done with the power of the Holy Spirit. Let's ask the Holy Spirit to help us see others' needs before our own, and remember the characteristics of the Perfect Shepherd as our role model.

Lord Jesus,

What an incredible role model You are for us, a Shepherd who is concerned about everyone and who laid his life down for each one of us, so we all can spend eternity in a land full of milk and honey. I pray we would desire to be just like You, and learn to put others first before ourselves. Holy Spirit, help us daily to walk as a good Shepherd and to become more God-centered.

"Sidetracked"

Proverbs 16:9

"A man's heart plans his way, but the Lord directs his steps."
– NIV

Having my destination planned, directions printed, I set out for my appointment. Running behind schedule, I began to stress about making it to my appointment on time. I hit every stoplight and fell further behind schedule. I followed the turn-by-turn directions and became lost.

Now even more frustrated, I backtracked to see if I had made a mistake on the directions and returned to the exact same spot a second time. Now I would be late for sure, and had to make the call to reschedule my appointment. Can you relate to my situation? It seemed no matter how hard I tried to get there, I could not get to my destination. But maybe there was a reason why I was to miss that appointment that never was rescheduled.

A close friend told me, " You can't steer a boat with the rudder if the boat is not moving." We can plan our course, but if we are not moving, we will remain in the exact same spot. The Lord will direct us according to His will, but we have to be moving in some direction. There are days I become so frustrated, trying to make things happen, when all I have to do is trust God's Word and step out in faith, and not be surprised when God sidetracks us to a new destination.

God has a perfect plan for all of us, and no matter how many wrong turns we make in life, He will eventually get us to our final destination. So if you are feeling lost, frustrated, and making circles in life, trust the Word of God, have peace in being lost right now, and know God will place you exactly where He wants you. All we have to remember to do is move, so the rudder can steer our boat.

Lord Jesus,

Thank You that we are lost and cannot find our way without You. I pray we would put all our trust in Your Word and stand on Your promises. Let us rejoice in being lost right now, knowing you have our final destinations in your Hands.

"Sliver of Sin"

Romans 6:11-12

"In the same way, count yourselves dead to sin but alive to God in Christ Jesus. Therefore do not let sin reign in your mortal body so that you obey its evil desires." - NIV

Romans 6:17 - 18

"But thanks be to God that, though you used to be slaves to sin, you wholeheartedly obeyed the form of teaching to which you were entrusted. You have been set free from sin and have become slaves to righteousness." - NIV

In charge of staining the quarter round to complete the week-long flooring project, staining the last solid oak piece, I suffered a long wooden sliver in my index finger. Immediately I removed it, thinking I got it out successfully. Finishing the project, I totally forgot about it.

A few days later, my finger had dramatically swollen up and looked infected. I felt my pulse quicken as I pressed and squeezed on the wounded finger. I examined the area of penetration and discovered part of the oak splinter had remained embedded deep in my finger. I could not see it with the visible eye, but knew it was in there. I attempted to dig it out, but my efforts were futile.

A few more days passed, and I noticed the swelling had gone down and the throbbing had subsided. I examined the wound again and noticed a small piece of wood at the entry point. My body excreted the piece of oak, knowing it did not belong there. My body over the past couple of days forced the infected splinter out of the wound, and once the piece of wood was removed, the finger started to heal.

Our body is described in the Bible as being a Holy Temple where the Holy Spirit resides once we accept Jesus as our Lord and Savior in our hearts. The moment we asked Jesus to come into our lives, all our past sin was forgotten forever, and we were made new in Christ.

If we allow sin to penetrate and remain in us, eventually we will suffer from a swollen, sin-filled wound. If we do not remove all of our sin immediately and forget about it, we will later discover that sin infecting us and causing some unnecessary pain. Our bodies were not designed to harbor sin, and the Holy Spirit will eventually convict us to repent and remove the sin once and for all.

Do you have a splinter of sin that you are ignoring, even though it has been throbbing and aching for some time now? You may not be able to see it with the eye, but you know it is there. Do not ignore it any longer. Ask Jesus for forgiveness and receive His healing blood. He will remove that sin from you like that infected splinter, and cast it away, never to remember it again.

To receive that healing blood, you have to have Jesus living in your heart. Nothing else can take away your sin, only the blood of Jesus Christ. If you do not have a personal relationship with Jesus, start one today. Simply pray to Him, tell Him that you are a sinner, ask Him to take your sin away, and believe He died for your sins and was raised to life from the grave. Ask Him to live in your heart and fill you with His Spirit, and give Him control of your life.

Lord Jesus,

Thank You that there is no sin too big to be removed, and one drop of your blood You shed at Calvary cleanses us of all unrighteousness. Thank You for living in each of our hearts and for giving us the Holy Spirit. I pray we would examine our lives closely and remove any sin we have forgotten about. I pray if there is anyone who reads this and does not have a personal relationship with You, they would pray a simple prayer and accept You forever, then talk to a local pastor about their decision.

"Tap Into The Power"

1 Corinthians2:4-5

"And my speech and my preaching was not with enticing words of man's wisdom, but in demonstration of the Spirit and of power: That your faith should not stand in the wisdom of men, but in the power of God." –NIV

Stepping into my high school physics class, I noticed a large lamp-shaped object sitting in the front of the class. Loud pops came from its interior, and two metal rods ran up the center. I knew it had to do with electricity, but in what capacity remained a mystery to me. The teacher explained the experiment briefly before going into detail about the object, its design, and its purpose.

After the half-hour lecture, minds loaded with information, we would now demonstrate what we learned. The class circled around the object and clasped hands. The teacher reached out and touched the object with his hand. Immediately, a surge of static electricity flowed from one hand to the other, forcing our hair to stand on end. I felt the electricity flow from the top of my head to the souls of my feet. The lights were turned off and you could see electricity flowing from hand to hand! I did not fully understand everything from the lecture, but to this day I remember to the detail the demonstration by feeling and experiencing it.

My pastor had an excellent analogy this weekend that relates. He said, "We as Christians tend to give Scripture for all situations, then back it with more Scripture, instead of stepping back and saying okay God, I did my part, it's all in your hands. I will trust you with the outcome no matter what it is." I personally find myself having faith in the Word, but a lack of faith concerning the power of Jesus Christ doing what He promised in His Word. The power of electricity is invisible, but with touch, it surges through you, demonstrating its power. Allowing Jesus to demonstrate His power through us will transform lives with experience, and not just words.

We are so accustomed to solving problems ourselves, and flood people with Scripture passage after Scripture passage when all we have to do is rely upon the true source of power and believe. It is easy to put our faith in the Word, but the challenge is standing on what the Word says, and believing the power of Christ will bring it to pass without us doing anything more. Just like the pastor said, "If it is of God it will stand, and if it is not of God it will pass." Most of the time, people do not remember everything said from the Word. But if we step back and allow God to demonstrate what He can do, they will be impacted for life.

Jesus was great at this in His ministry on Earth. He would use the Word of God to teach and help people, but would demonstrate His power so people would remember. There is nothing wrong with the Word, but at times we can overdo it. We need to follow Jesus' example and use the Word to help people, but allow the power of Christ to work in their lives. Life-changing experiences will be remembered forever. Jesus told us we would do greater things than He did. Believe you can heal the sick, make the blind see, allow the lame to walk, and even raise the dead! It is all done through the power of Jesus that flows from the top of your head to the soles of your feet. Extend past the Word and tap into the power!

Lord Jesus,

Thank You for coming to the earth, not just teaching, but demonstrating Your power. Thank You that you made it possible to do mighty things through Your name. I pray we would tap into the power of Your name and let it surge through us, and boldly demonstrate the power in Your name to those you place in our paths.

"The Challenging Hill"

Psalm 23:4

"Yea, though I walk through the valley of the shadow of death, I will fear no evil: for thou art with me; thy rod and thy staff comfort me."
– KJV

Turning the bend, gaining momentum on a downhill slope, I looked ahead to see what lay ahead of me. At first it did not look challenging, but midway up the hill, my perspective quickly changed. I shifted into a higher gear to maintain my forward speed, but changing gears did not produce the results I was looking for. My legs began to burn and my side ached, as I could not gain my second wind. The hill looked endless and the thought of turning around and ending my ride looked inviting to me.

The highest gear was no match for this hill, and it was going to take everything I had to conquer this long stretch of road. Moving slowly up the hill, almost at a standstill, I leaned forward, shifting all my weight to my legs. I could feel the torque on the crank, and the front tire began to lift, forcing me to lean forward more and more. Beads of sweat poured from my brow and I was out of breath. Every part of me burned with pain, but I was determined to make it to the top. It took me several grueling minutes, constantly pedaling without stopping, but I made it and lived to tell the story.

It reminds me of life. We can be cruising along, gaining momentum, and suddenly be faced with an uphill challenge. Those situations cause us to flip through our gears, trying to do everything in our power, but we quickly discover we are no match for the mountain we face. The important thing to remember is not to give up, even if every part of your body is burning with pain. Jesus promises us in His Word He will get us through no matter how high or how dark the journey is. He will take us through tests and trials to shape us and mold us for His glory.

Beads of blood poured from the brow of Jesus as He carried his cross uphill to Calvary. He did not stop, and there were times when He was at a standstill and out of breath, yet He continued the journey with everything in Him, for us. The weight of the cross lay heavy on his back, forcing Him to lean forward more and more. He burned with pain, but was determined to make it to the top and die for you and me. So the next time you are faced with a challenging hill, remember what Jesus went through for you, and know He will get you through. Do not give up, lean forward, and pedal harder.

Lord Jesus,

Thank You for not giving up. Thank You for enduring the pain that ran through Your body to accomplish the task at hand. I pray we would look at Your strength to get us through hard times and those uphill challenges. I pray we would put all our faith and trust in You to get us through the dark valleys, for Your glory.

"The Curse"

[ornament]

Romans 3:24-25

"Being justified freely by his grace through the redemption that is in Christ Jesus: Whom God hath set forth to be propitiation through faith in his blood, to declare his righteousness for the remission of sins that are past, through the forbearance of God." – NIV

W e can all recall a time of being chased down, tagged, and hearing "You now have the cooties." We became cursed, and the kids playing with us did not want anything to do with us until the start of a new game. Of course this was and still is today a childhood game, but the point I want to make is that we received the curse from Adam and Eve, sinning against God, but God does not see us having cooties and still wants our sinful souls to spend eternity in heaven with Him.

It doesn't sound fair, does it? Adam and Eve fell, and all generations that have existed, including future generations, will be tagged with the curse. But God loves us so much that He gave His only Son to die for us to bridge the gap and allow his Son's blood, only the blood of Jesus, to atone for our past, present, and future sins.

God made a second blood covenant with His creation, and this time no animals would have to be sacrificed. No more walking in the blood alley, no more altars, and no need to make a covenant scar for all to see. This will be and is the last covenant God will make with His children. Jesus' blood is our last hope to be washed from all our cooties.

God does not want to see His children's souls lost forever in the eternal torment of hell. God wants all His children to be in blood covenant with Him. Through this covenant, we become joint heirs to Jesus and receive His grace and favor freely. We are weak in our flesh (bodies) and we can find strength in the covenant with Jesus Christ. This covenant was made to combine our weakness with God's strength to form a lasting union.

Do you realize we have everything Jesus has because we are joint heirs with Him? We have an incredible power source to tap into, and through faith we have everything we need to survive in this world. He told us in His Word we would do greater things than He did while on earth, through the Holy Spirit given to us as our comforter.

When the Apostle Paul said, "Having done all the standing, stand with the armor of God, stand in the blood of Christ," he is instructing us to stand in the covenant with Jesus and draw upon the strength he gives us. Just look what Paul went through while he was on this earth. God will stand with us and not break his promises to us. The blessing of the covenant can be attained through faith, and faith comes by hearing, and hearing by the Word of God.

The scars on Jesus' brow, hands, feet, side, and back represent the new covenant we have with God. He is the bridge between the curse and the blessings of God. All we have to do is walk across the bridge in faith. God desires that we all walk through the blood of His Son, Jesus Christ, because he wants to bless all His children. Through the blood, we can do all things through Christ who strengthens us!

God wants to give us the desires of our hearts, but before He can do that, we must remain in covenant with Him. His Word instructs us to love him with all our hearts, with all our minds, and all our souls. He wants us to live by His Word and trust in His Word. He has given us a life manual to use while on this earth. We can find all the answers to our problems there.

Jesus is chasing you today, but does not want to give you the cooties. Instead, He wants to pass His blessings to you. Accept Jesus into your life, give Him control of everything in your life, and walk in covenant with Him by faith, trusting Him with your life. He will provide your every need, so get rid of the curse and claim the blessing!

Lord Jesus,

Thank You for breaking the curse and setting us free through Your blood on the cross. All we had to do was freely receive the gift of eternal life simply by calling, believing, and trusting on Your name. I pray we would just be reminded what You did for us to break the curse and set us free. In our freedom is were the blessings lay and it is my prayer we would stay in the blessing.

"The Golden Ticket"

Psalm 36:8-9

"They feast on the abundance of your house; you give them drink from your river of delights. For with you is the fountain of life; in your light we see light." - NIV

Oने of my favorite movies of all time has been *Willy Wonka and the Chocolate Factory*. I have dreamed of finding the golden ticket hidden in one of the five Wonka bars, and I have imagined mountains bursting with sugar, rivers flowing with chocolate, and experiencing Wonka's wild inventions. Who would not want to meet Willy Wonka and the busy Oompa-Loompas?

Willy Wonka and the Chocolate Factory was filmed in 1971. Yahoo Movies describe it as an amusing musical about a world famous candy maker who hides five golden tickets in candy bars for five lucky children. Young, good-natured Charlie (Peter Ostrum) wins one of the tickets hidden amongst thousands of Wonka chocolate bars.

What did Charlie and the other four kids win? A tour through Willy Wonka's chocolate factory, led by a lovable, eccentric, but often mean-spirited Wonka (Gene Wilder). The factory itself is like a fantasy world: crazy color schemes, wild inventions, secret rooms, and lots and lots of delectable sweets.

Mr. Wonka gives strict instructions to obey his rules, and during the tour he tests each child's character and honesty. All of the children fail. One falls into the chocolate river, another turns into a large blueberry, a third tried to steal a golden egg, and one child thought he was on TV, only to discover he would be reduced in size.

Charlie and his grandfather were tested, and they thought Mr. Wonka was not aware of the soda pop they drank, making them lighter than air. Belching and burping was the thing that saved them from being sucked up in the ventilation shaft. Mr. Wonka confronted Charlie with his act of disobedience, and through repentance and surrender of the one thing Mr. Wonka gave the children (a piece of candy), Charlie passed the test. He was awarded the chocolate factory! Charlie walked in poor, and in the end was given the ultimate golden ticket.

God wants to give us a golden ticket, and only wants the best for His children. He gives His Word for us to obey and He will test our obedience. He sees all that we do, even when we try to hide behind closed doors. When we do fail, His grace, mercy, and forgiveness will restore us. Finally, if we place our trust and hope in the Lord, we can claim the promises of his Word. So, feast, drink, and live for God!

Lord Jesus,

Thank You for giving the greatest resource of all time, the Bible. It is our golden ticket to staying on the right path in obedience to You. Your word is a lamp to our feet and directs our path. I pray we would meditate and memorize Your word daily, for those times we get onto the wrong path, which could lead us into a mess in our lives. I pray we would cling on to Your word like Charlie did when he found the last golden ticket.

"The True Sacrifice"

Matthew 27:50-53

"Jesus, when he cried again with a loud voice, yielded up the ghost. And, behold the veil of the temple was rent in twain from the top to the bottom; and the earth did quake, and the rocks rent; and the graves were opened; and many bodies of the saints which slept arose, and came out of the graves after his resurrection, and went into the holy city, and appeared unto many." - KJV

Imagine what it was like, being an Israelite in the Old Testament. You patiently watch Moses build this tent structure, and hear rumors of God coming to live with you. "What is Moses up to now?" You may be thinking, "Haven't we been through enough already?" You watch Moses make the finishing touch to the courtyard around what was now called the tabernacle, and hear an announcement that everyone is to attend a meeting Moses is organizing. "What is he going to do or show us now?" Then you are just informed the Lord will appear before the Israelites in eight days.

Eight days later, you gather with everyone in the courtyard of the tabernacle, and notice Aaron leading a bull calf and ram to the altar. Aaron announces, "Take a male goat for a sin offering, a calf and a lamb - both a year old, without defect - for a burnt offering, and an ox and a ram for a fellowship offering to sacrifice before the Lord, together with a grain offering mixed with oil. For the Lord will appear to you today." You watch as Aaron begins the atonement ceremony, and the sacrifices begin. Several animals are led to the altar to be slaughtered for the Lord. Aaron is meticulous in every step of the process as he follows the instructions God gave to Moses.

After Aaron finishes with the sin offering, the burnt offering, and the fellowship offering, he steps down and goes into the Tent of Meeting with Moses. As you stand there in silence, waiting for Moses and Aaron to return, you begin to wonder what it will be like to see the Lord. You hear someone say, "Look, it's Moses and Aaron coming from the tent." Your eyes are now glued to their every move, anticipating the Lord's arrival. A cloud appears suddenly and fire consumes the burnt offering and the fat portions on the altar. All the people around you shout for joy! Instantly everyone is facedown in awe of God.

Burnt offering, grain offering, sin offering, guilt offering, ordination offering, and the fellowship offering, all these were regulations the Israelites had to perform to be in the presence of the Lord. Can you imagine if we had to follow all those regulations today? Every year we would gather at the altar and sacrifice several animals before God, and all our sins would be cast on a scapegoat to be set free in the wilderness. Do you realize the ultimate sacrifice was given to us as a gift, and has atoned for all our sin past, present, and future? Jesus Christ, the perfect, unblemished lamb, died for you and me on the cross at Calvary. I quote from the Promise Keepers Bible, "Jesus did not enter into God's presence by means of the blood of goats and calves; but He entered the Most Holy Place once for all by His own blood, having obtained eternal redemption."

No matter what we have done, Jesus wants one drop of His blood to atone for us. All we have to do is confess our sins to God, and believe by faith Jesus died for you and me. His blood is the ultimate and only sacrifice that will wash away any sin in our lives. We just need to allow Jesus to come into our lives and take over. There is nothing humanly possible we can do to get into heaven. There is only one way, and that way is Jesus. He wants to invade our lives with His love, mercy, and grace. We will never be perfect in God's eyes, but we can be near perfect by living a righteous life before God. We are going to fail Jesus every day, but if we confess our sins to God, He will cast our sins into the deepest ocean and forget them forever. Does that mean we can sin every day and get away with sin? No! We must turn from our evil ways and seek righteousness with all our hearts. We can do this every day with the help of the Holy Spirit that lives in our hearts. Just remember what Jesus did for us, and take each day moment by moment. Jesus is and will be the only sacrifice we need to atone for our sins past, present, and future.

Lord Jesus,

Thank You for being our true sacrifice, the perfect lamb, who ministered your unconditional love, grace, and mercy in the flesh, and

You continue that practice today through your Spirit. You are our perfect sacrifice, as there is no other like You. I pray we would lift Your name and praise You for the act You did just because You love us and want us to spend eternity with You. I pray if there are any who do not know You, they would receive the free gift You have for them of eternal life.

"Was It All Worth It?"

Romans 3:23-25

"For all have sinned, and come short of the glory of God; Being justified freely by his grace through the redemption that is in Christ Jesus: Whom God hath set forth to be a propitiation through faith in his blood, to declare his righteousness for the remission of sins that are past, through the forbearance of God." - KJV

2 Corinthians 3:17

*"Now the Lord is the Spirit, and where the Spirit of the Lord is, there is **freedom**."* - NIV

Galatians 5:1

*"For **freedom** Christ has set us free; stand fast therefore, and do not submit again to a yoke of slavery."* - NIV

Bloodstained lands, screams of war from the east to west, men and women dying for one common cause, and I ask you, "Was it all worth it?" Some died not getting the opportunity to see the promise of freedom, and some survived and lived or live in peace. We have freedom today because brave warriors drenched in honor took an oath to fight and die for our country. Today is Veterans' Day, and we need to take a moment of silence to honor all those who served and those who died for our freedom.

A couple days ago, in a phone conversation, my mother told me "When your father returned home form Viet Nam, our country did not honor him or the men that returned that day." How did those men and women feel the moment they stepped off the plane, with no formal reception, and no flags waving? I bet some of them were asking the question, "Was it all worth it?" Men have sacrificed their lives for centuries and continue to this day, but there was one sacrifice that can give us true freedom!

Bloodstained cross, the ultimate sacrifice. Jesus Christ knew His death was worth it. His screams of pain and death on the cross have given us freedom, if we only will believe He died, rose from the grave, and lives today. Jesus is a warrior and brought honor to his father by dying for our sins. I can only imagine how Jesus felt, having the nails pierce his hands and feet, the crown of thorns penetrating His scalp, and the dehydration flowing through his failing body. I bet Jesus looked down from the cross with tears in his eyes, watching people turn their backs and leave Him to die, not knowing what He was doing for them.

Those who believe He died for them can live in freedom, knowing we have a place in eternity with Him. I am sure He still sheds tears for those who continue to turn their backs on Him. All of creation will stand before Christ and He will say, "My good and faithful servant, great will be your reward," or "Away from me, I did not know you." What will you hear on that day from Him? It is not too late to know Jesus as your personal Savior, secure your name in Heaven, and begin living for Him today.

Some of us will die not getting the opportunity to see the promised land, and some will have the opportunity to experience true freedom and live in peace where there will be no death, no tears, and no worries. Those who do not choose to accept Christ as their Savior will be separated from God forever, and I ask you, "Will it be worth it?" God is calling all His children to honor Him and become warriors for His Kingdom. He desires all of His creation to accept Jesus, so the choice is yours.

Lord Jesus,

Thank You for the freedom we have in You. As Christians, we know the only one we have to impress is You, and nothing else really matters. We know You desire all to be saved and none to be lost. I pray hell would be empty and heaven would be over-populated. Sometimes we can take our freedom for granted, so help us to keep everything in perspective, according to Your will.

"Watching"

John 5:19-20

"Jesus gave them this answer: 'I tell you the truth, the Son can do nothing by himself; he can do only what he sees his Father doing, **because whatever the Father does the Son also does.** *For the Father loves the Son and shows him all he does. Yes, to your amazement he will show him even greater things than these.'"* NIV

My eyes were glued to his every move, and I would immediately duplicate any movement he made. I stood like him, matching his posture to a tee. My grip was exactly the same as his and when he changed something, I did, too. I was determined to be just like my dad and become a great fisherman that day.

My father knew I was imitating him, and at times had me scratching my head, waving my arm, and hopping up and down. I thought it was all part of fishing. When he started laughing, I knew something was up, but I saw my father as the greatest fisherman who ever lived, and nothing would convince me differently. Needless to say, I did not catch a darn thing that day, but neither did he.

Christians have a Father in Heaven who desires His children to see Him as their role model and imitate Him here on Earth. I wonder, if Jesus walked among us today, how would we act? Would we imitate His every move and desire to be just like Him, or would we not even notice Him? Would we consider Him the greatest fisherman to ever live and nothing could convince us differently?

Two points I would like to make. First, Jesus does walk with us daily in the Spirit and knows our every move. He knows what we do behind closed doors when no one is looking. He desires our actions, words, and thoughts to bring glory to Him. Jesus Christ lives in us and wants to shine through us to this world. We must keep our eyes on Jesus and desire to be like Him so people can see Christ in us.

Second, Fathers and Mothers, know that your children are watching your every move. They look upon you as their hero and knight in shining armor. They will imitate their role models. If you wave your arm, jump up and down, or scratch your head, they will, too. Keep in mind, good habits breed godly children, and bad habits breed destruction. Remember, you are always being watched by Jesus Christ and by those around you, especially your children.

Lord Jesus,

Thank You for being the perfect role model. Thank You for never leaving us nor forsaking us and always walking with us. I pray we would model after You and desire to be just like You. I pray that fathers and mothers would be good role models for their children and know their children are watching their every move.

"Can't Fly Before Its Time"

Deuteronomy 28:12

"The Lord shall open unto thee his good treasure, the heaven to give the rain unto thy land in his season, and to bless all the work of thine hand: and thou shalt lend unto many nations, and thou shalt not borrow." – KJV

My uncle felt something climbing up his leg in the car. He had no clue what it was, but quickly found out. He carefully scooped the insect off his leg while driving in the car, and upon returning from the store, placed it on his porch railing for all of us to observe. We quickly noticed it could not fly and was throwing its body weight around, flopping from side to side, eventually falling to the ground. Its wings looked wet and rolled, as if it recently hatched.

I asked, "How did that get in your car, Chuck?"

My uncle replied, "There must have been a cocoon hidden in my car somewhere."

We all edged in to examine the insect and assess the situation. We decided to put it on the back of a lawn chair, so it could hang and dry in the sun and not become bird food. It clung to the chair and immediately calmed down, as if it knew its limitations of flight. The moth had to wait patiently for its wings to dry before it could venture into the new world.

I have a difficult time with patience, and like the moth, want my wings to dry fast, so I can fly. I find myself flopping around, anxious and worried at times. Can you relate? Many times I have tried to fly under my own strength, without God, resulting in a quick crash to the ground. The Lord has a close eye on us, and only wants the best for His children. He wants us to be patient and trust in Him and in His timing. He will notify us when our wings are dry enough for flight and will give us the confidence to fully stretch out our wings to fly.

God does not want us flying with wet wings, He wants us to be whole and prepared to take on the assignment He gives us. So if you feel like you are hanging out to dry, keep positive, because one day soon, you will be soaring.

Lord Jesus,

Thank You for your promises You give in Your word. Thank You we can place all our trust and hope into one source, and know You will open your treasure to us in Your perfect time. I pray we would have the patience to wait on You and not try to fly before our wings fully dry and develop.

"What's Your Wish?"

I Kings 2:11

"And God said unto him, Because thou hast asked this thing, and hast not asked for thyself long life; neither hast asked riches for thyself, nor hast asked for the life of thine enemies; but hast asked for thyself understanding to discern judgment." – KJV

If the LORD appeared to you in a dream and said, "Ask what I shall give thee," what would your reply be? Immediately, several things come to my mind, like financial freedom, a huge house, and luxury cars. There is nothing wrong with those things, but we cannot fall into the trap of worshiping them over God. Jesus wants us to seek Him and the Kingdom first, and rely upon Him to give us everything else as needed. Solomon proved this to us by denying material wealth and power in exchange for wisdom.

Solomon could have asked for anything, but chose to ask for understanding and discernment. We may be thinking, "What the heck were you thinking, Solomon? I would have made my wish wide and deep." Now, you cannot tell me if someone approached you and said, "I will give you whatever you want, just whisper it in my ear, and it is yours," would you reply, "I would like some wisdom and understanding, please"?

It reminds me of the show in the 70s called *Let's Make a Deal.* If you are not familiar with the concept of the show, let me briefly explain. The contestant would be faced with a decision to trade in what they just won for what was behind doors 1, 2, or 3. Some times a trade would be rewarded with a larger, more expensive prize and other times the result would be a booby prize, worth much less.

Solomon was faced with an important decision and decided to hang on to what God was going to give him, and not trade it for the world. I have to say, I would not have asked for wisdom or understanding, but for material gain. Can you relate? What are we putting first in our lives? We think having everything would solve all our problems, but in reality it only leads to the booby prize behind Door Number 3.

Let's see what the Lord said to Solomon in 1Kings 3:12, based on the choice he made: Behold, I have done according to thy words: lo, I have given thee a wise and an understanding heart. But look what he said in verse 13: And I have also given thee that which thou hast not asked, both riches, and honor: so that there shall not be any among the kings like unto thee all thy days.

If we, like Solomon, seek Jesus first over everything else in our lives, we can walk away with the total showcase. If we can learn to seek the Kingdom first and trust Jesus with the rest, we will not get stuck with something we can't use (booby prize). Instead, we can walk in the strength of Jesus and trust He will give us the riches and desires of our hearts.

Lord Jesus,

Thank You for wisdom and understanding. Thank You for giving us the desires of our hearts, according to Your will. I pray we would hold onto Your Word and promises, and not trade them in for the world. I pray we would seek You first in everything we do and trust You with our lives.

"Who Am I?"

Matthew 16:24-25

"Then said Jesus unto his disciples, If any man will come after me, let him deny himself, and take up his cross, and follow me. For whosoever will save his life shall lose it: and whosoever will lose his life for my sake will find it." - KJV

Waking from a deep sleep, mouth dry, I did not know who or where I was. Within a few moments, I gained perspective on things and realized I was only dreaming. I lay silent in my bed and began to think about the dream and how it related to my life. In the dream, everyone was faceless and wore the same black suit. We were all walking in a maze, taking different turns, only to find dead end after dead end. Everyone in my dream seemed to be chasing something, bumping into each other and leaving the dead end paths with nothing in their hands No one was able to escape the endless walls of this maze.

The Lord has been asking me to give over everything to Him, and of course I rationalize and think maybe if I hang on to this one thing in my life, he will not mind. Why is it so hard to surrender every area of our lives to Christ? I believe the Lord was telling me something in that dream, and deep in my heart, I know what it is. Every day, the Lord has been showing me what I need to surrender over to Him and I reply, "Why Lord?" After reading a book written by John Eldredge entitled, *Waking The Dead,* the Lord laid on my heart the question, "Who am I?"

"Take up your cross daily and walk with me", the Lord tells me. I am bigger than any maze and you have no need to chase dead ends. The Lord's Word tells us to **"Trust in the Lord with all of your heart, and lean not on your own understanding. In all your ways acknowledge Him, and He will make your paths straight."** Proverbs 3 5-6

Why is it so difficult to trust with all our heart? Have you ever gotten the sick feeling in your stomach, doubt racing through your mind, allowing the devil to feed you a bunch of lies? The Lord wants us to trust Him with all areas of our lives. All areas.

Like me, what are you holding onto in your own strength? What is God telling you to release, and what lies have you believed from the devil? Life was not meant to be easy, but Jesus can navigate us through the maze of life. He may lead us into a dead end, but it is only to teach us and mold us. John teaches us in his book to ask ourselves to write down five words that describe our lives. What five words immediately surface in your mind?

Jesus tells me and you today, "Know who I am." Greater is he who is in me than he who is in the world. I urge you to be crucified with Christ. Do not live for your own gain, but live for Christ and His Kingdom. Honor, Love, Worship, and Trust Jesus! He wants all of us, not just some of us, as we were created for a specific purpose: to bring Him glory. When you find yourself walking in the faceless, confusing maze of life, remember there is a way out! I encourage you not to worry about your life, how successful, how accepted, how powerful you may be. Just know that none of that matters, and the only thing Jesus is calling us to do is surrender and to trust Him with all our heart.

Lord Jesus,

Thank You for being our cornerstone and the rock we can cling to for strength and protection. Thank You for the promises we have in Your Word to live by and apply to our lives daily. I pray we would die to ourselves, crucify our flesh, and pick up our cross to follow You, no matter where that may lead, as we know You only desire to give us abundant life here on Earth. May we choose to loose our lives daily while seeking You first.

"Why Worry?"

Luke 12:28-31

"If then God so clothe the grass, which is today in the field, and tomorrow is cast into the oven; how much more will he clothe you, O ye of little faith? And seek not ye what ye shall eat, or what ye shall drink, neither be ye of doubtful mind. For all these things do the nations of the world seek after: and your Father knoweth that ye have a need of these things. But rather seek ye the kingdom of God; and all these things shall be added unto you." - KJV

Imagine with me for a moment, how awesome it would have been to be one of the twelve disciples Jesus picked to minister with for three years. Huddled around the Master and Teacher to hear His wise words. Eyes glued to His lips, ears tuned to His every word, and hearts being moved in ways like never before. Each time Jesus would call His disciples to gather, He had something very important to say to them, and wanted them to live by His example.

Just think about walking with Jesus when He was here on earth over two thousand years ago. If Jesus came to me and said, "Follow me," I would have dropped everything I was doing in a heartbeat to learn from the Master. I would have recorded every word and became like a sponge, soaking up His knowledge and wisdom. Learning from Him and applying His teaching to my life and witness. Why do I have a problem doing that in my walk with Him today? Why, at times, can I see myself being a man of little faith?

In Luke chapter 12, verses 22 through 34, Jesus tells us not to worry about our life, to trust with faith that our futures are secure in Him, and those who do not listen to His teaching are men of little faith. It is so easy to worry and be anxious about our lives and futures. Jesus said, "Who of you by worrying can add a single hour to his or her life? Since you cannot do this very little thing, why do you worry about the rest?"

Why is it so hard at times to trust in something that we cannot see? What are you worrying about today? Health, wealth, job, family, or your future in general? I have noticed one thing in my short walk with Jesus: He has never failed me yet, and provided for my every need, yet I still worry about things. Can you relate to this? Jesus is the same as he was when He ministered to the disciples on

Earth, and expects us to trust in His wisdom and teaching because everything comes from the Father. He wants us to trust only in Him and not in ourselves.

God continues to remind me to turn to Luke 12:31, " But seek His Kingdom and these things will be given to you as well." Be encouraged with me to surrender all areas of our lives to Christ. God desires that we be faithful, trust, and allow Him to show us how much He loves His children through His provisions.

Let's change our hearts today and allow God to show us how much He loves us. He wants control of our lives, all areas, as nothing is hidden from God's eyes. He wants to know what we treasure. He tells us through His Word, "For where your treasure is, there your heart will be also." Join with me to replace worry, anxiety, and our futures with the treasure of Jesus Christ, because He desires to be number one in your heart! Know that you do not need to worry about anything, because the Father is pleased to give you His Kingdom.

Lord Jesus,

Thank You that all we need is Your Word. We do not need to worry about what we are going to eat, drink or anything else, other than focusing on seeking the kingdom first. We have Your promise in Your Word that you know our every need and desire in our heart. I pray we would stop relying on the things of the world and rely one hundred percent on You. Help us to surrender the things we have failed to give to You, and replace them with a desire according to Your will.

"Wild At Heart"

Ezekiel 18:31

"Cast away from you all your transgressions, whereby ye have transgressed; and make you a new heart and a new spirit: for why will ye die, O house of Israel?" – KJV

1 Peter 3:4

"But let it be the hidden man of the heart, in that which is not corruptible, even the ornament of a meek and quite spirit, which is in the sight of God of great price." - KJV

Reflecting back on my childhood, I yearn for some of the characteristics I had as a child, and have recently started to regain. I can recall the time I would pick up a stick and pretend it was my machine gun, sword, and rocket launcher. In my imaginary world, I would be surrounded by hundreds of enemy soldiers closing in all around me. My heart would be pumping a hundred miles a minute, and my energy level would soar through the roof. I was prepared to take on the world with my stick, and nothing was going to stop me!

What happened to me? For several years, I have been hiding behind a rock like a scared rabbit. A shell of a man, afraid to take on the world, I became comfortable with my life. My heart became cold, as the fire of adventure once within burned out. Fear had taken over, and the little boy that could take on the world with his stick died. Just recently, God has shown me that I have been a cowardly lion, and that is not what he designed me to be. He wants to change my heart so I can become a mighty lion and roar for His kingdom.

I am reading a book called *The Journey of Desire: Searching for the Life We've Only Dreamed Of,* by John Eldredge. In chapter eight, he outlines what a mate is looking for in a man. A woman desires a warrior, a man of honor, willing to take on the world for her! She wants a man with a wild heart full of desire and endless love, willing to sacrifice his life for her. Song of Songs reflects this: "Listen! My Lover! Look! Here he comes, leaping across the mountains, bounding over the hills. My lover is like a gazelle or a young stag. (2:8-9)

It is time to wake up those dead hearts and fill them with adventure, then rescue our beauty and draw her into the adventure that brings her heart alive! Let me ask you a question: Are you doing something that makes you come alive? Do you feel alive, or are you comfortable with life? Think back when you were a child. What adventure did you take on? What set your heart on fire? Eugene Peterson reminds us that life is a battle and journey. He quotes, "Life is not a game of striving and indulgence. It is not a long march of duty and obligation. You must take the journey of desire, we have to get our hearts back, which means getting our desire back."

We are made in the image of God; we carry within us the desire for our true life of intimacy and adventure. It is time to pick up those imaginary sticks and take on the world for Christ! Let honor, integrity, and love flow from your heart and bless those around you. I will close with what C.S Lewis says: " We are half-hearted creatures, fooling about with drink and sex and ambition, when infinite joy is offered us, like an ignorant child who wants to go on making mud pies in a slum because he cannot imagine what is meant by the offer of a holiday at the sea. We are too easily pleased."

I know that's not our heart. That is not the person God wants us to be. Listen to the promise of God to us: "I will give you a new heart and put a new spirit in you; I will remove from you your heart of stone and give you a heart of flesh." (Ezekiel 36:26 NIV)

Lord Jesus,

Thank You for living in our hearts and making our hearts wild for You. It is your Spirit that sustains us and gives us life. I pray we would strive each day to find the adventure that makes our hearts come alive for You. Let our wild hearts bring glory only to You.

"Actions Speak Louder Than Words"

James 2:14 - 17

"What good is it, my brothers, if a man claims to have faith but has no deeds? Can such faith save him? Suppose a brother or sister is without clothes and daily food. If one of you says to him, "Go, I wish you well; keep warm and well fed," but does nothing about his physical needs, what good is it? In the same way, faith by itself, if it is not accompanied by action, is dead." - NIV

I arrived downtown early to help set up and prepare to feed the home-less. It was a very brisk winter day, as the temperatures dipped into the teens and the wind chill cut to the bone. I stepped out of my truck, and within a few minutes, I could feel the cold penetrating my fingers and toes. I continued to fight off the freezing temperatures by staying busy unloading tables and chairs, setting up a station to hand out winter clothing, and helping prepare the food line.

The steam from the hot food rose in the air like an industrial smoke stack. People began to form a line to receive a free meal, but most gathered at the table for a ration of warm clothing. We explained there would be a process and everyone would eat a warm meal before we handed out clothing. I could not help but notice all the people around me in great need, as most were not prepared for the winter. They were bundled in several layers of clothing, some had socks on their hands, and plastic bags wrapped around their shoes.

The hot plates of food acted as temporary hand warmers, and some of the homeless just wanted a cup of hot coffee to use as a heat source. The little children's cheeks and noses were red like freshly bloomed roses. Their cries echoed deep in my heart, and there was nothing I could do but pray for them. My heart began to break and moisture filled my eyes as I witnessed all of God's creation in need. We did everything we could to make sure everyone had received a warm meal, a ration of clothing, and the love of Christ through our actions, words, and prayers.

There was not enough warm clothing to go around, and many did not receive anything. I cried out to the Lord in my Spirit to use me in helping in anyway I could. The desire in my heart was to clothe everyone there and to provide proper shelter for those with no place to lay their heads. Faced with reality, I could not begin to make an impact and thought, "What difference can I make?" Just then, the Lord introduced me to a man who came up to me, stared into my eyes, and did not have to say a word.

The Spirit of the Lord gave me the peace to surrender my winter coat, gloves, and ear warmers to this man. The compassion I felt towards him was so strong in Christ, and I did not think twice as I handed him my winter clothing in faith. I helped him put on the coat, slipping it over the layers of thin shirts he wore. His hands were like ice when I touched them to help place the gloves over his fingers, and his ears were blue from the cold as I watched him place the ear warmers carefully over them. His eyes filled with tears, and he smiled and walked away.

The Lord desires we be his hands and feet anywhere we are. We have to be open to listening to the Holy Spirit and doing what we feel in our spirit by faith. The Lord provides everything we need, and we can have faith that we will always be provided for, no matter what. The Lord will place people in need in our paths, and we have to be willing to give what belongs to the Lord to those in need. Make sure you have a total peace about giving, because nothing dealing with confusion is from the Lord. We have to remember everything we have is the Lord's, and we must be willing to sow our time, resources, and money to further the Kingdom of God and show those in need the love of Christ.

I had to retreat many times to my truck for warmth, and a fellow Christian had given me a scarf to wrap around my neck, but the warmth of Christ in my heart melted away the cold. I can still see that man's tear-filled eyes and smile in my mind, and I thank the Lord for my obedience to be the hands and feet of Jesus on a cold winter day. Remember, faith is proven through our actions, not with empty words of encouragement or promises. So let our actions speak louder than our words.

Lord Jesus,

Thanks You for providing everything we will ever need, so we do not have to worry about our lives, about what we will eat, wear, or where we will sleep. I pray we would let our actions speak louder than words, and have the faith to do what You call us to do. I pray our hearts would go out to those in need, and boldly share the love of Christ in a practical way.

"My Mother"

Proverbs 31:28

"Her children arise up, and call her blessed; her husband also, and he praiseth her." - KJV

I realized something today. I realized my mother is a Proverbs 31 woman. I would like to break down the chapter by verses, and show you some similar characteristics of my mother. How appropriate this is for Mother's Day. Some mothers do not get the respect they deserve, and I would like to show you that being a mother is a position of honor in the Lord's eyes. To all the mothers in the world, my hat is off to you in deepest respect and love in Christ.

Proverbs 31:10 *A wife of noble character who can find? She is worth far more than rubies.*

Verse 11-12 says, *Her husband has full confidence in her and lacks nothing of value. She brings him good, not harm, all the days of her life.* My mother and father have been married for 46 years, and my mother has brought nothing but good things to him, with nothing but honor and respect. I notice when they are together how they look at each other, how their love has grown deeper and stronger with time, and how they finish each other's sentences or even thoughts.

Verse 13-15: *She selects wool and flax and works with eager hands. She is like the merchant ships, bringing her food from afar. She gets up while it is still dark; she provides food for her family and portions for her servant girls.* I can recall many times waking up to the smell of pancakes on the griddle, the sizzling bacon aroma lingering in the air, and to top off everything, the fresh smell of biscuits filling my nose. She would always be up before dawn, serving her family in love with her cooking, and our lunches were always packed ready to go. She made sure we were presentable and mentally prepared for the day ahead.

Verse 16-18: *She considers a field and buys it; out of her earnings she plants a vineyard. She sets about her work vigorously; her arms are strong for her tasks. She sees that her trading is profitable, and her lamp does not go out at night.* I recall when my mom worked a few odd jobs while being a full-time stay-home mother, and she saved every penny of her earnings in a Christmas fund for her family. She would burn the midnight oil in prayer after she knew her children were tucked safely in bed for the night. She would always be there, 24x7, if we called out in sickness or were awakened by a bad dream.

Verse 19-21: *In her hand she holds the distaff and grasps the spindle with her fingers. She opened her arms to the poor and extends her hands to the needy. When it snows, she has no fear for her household; for all of them are clothed in scarlet.* My mother was the queen of mending holes in our clothes, and she used her creative talents to custom design some of the things we wore. Like the blue jean hats with our names embroidered on them that we wore while touring in Germany. She would drop everything to help her family. To this day, she still reaches out to the poor and needy, putting other people's needs before her own. She has always been a true example of a servant to her family and community. I think she went overboard at times, making sure we were warm in our six layers of clothes during the winter months.

Verse 22-24: *She makes coverings for her bed; she is clothed in fine linen and purple. Her husband is respected at the city gate, where he takes his seat among the elders of the land. She makes linen garments and sells them, and supplies the merchants with sashes.* My mother has never been into materialism, but she has not lacked in anything, as my father is an excellent provider. I recall seeing how beautiful my mother was and still is today, how she has always taken good care of herself and her family. She has stood at my father's side to this day, and you can see the respect she has for her warrior. My father is well respected in the community and their union is viewed as a marriage made in heaven.

Verse 25-28: *She is clothed with strength and dignity; she can laugh at the days to come. She speaks with wisdom, and faithful instruction is on her tongue. She watches over the affairs of her household and does not eat the bread of idleness. Her children arise and call her blessed; her husband also, and he praises her.*

My mother seems to have a smile stretching from ear to ear, always full of joy and happiness. She would be there to lift our spirits when we were down about something. She has always been strong in her faith, and when Mom talked, we listened, or we would be introduced to a warm, firm hand. When my father was away, she ruled the roost with wisdom, integrity, and love pouring from her lips. My family loves our mother, and I do not know what we would do without her. She never slows down, always on the move, serving others.

Verse 29-31: *"Many women do noble things, but you surpass them all." Charm is deceptive, and beauty is fleeting; but a woman who fears the Lord is to be praised. Give her the reward she has earned, and let her works bring praise at the city gate.* My mother has never been about anything the world defines a mother to be; instead she has defined and demonstrated her motherhood on the Word of God. I remember almost wetting my pants the first time I laid eyes on my mother with a mud facial and a towel wrapped around her head. As my mother grows older, her beauty only grows stronger to me, and I can see Christ beaming through her eyes and heart. For as long as I can remember, my mother has always been about her family and dedicated to one heart, my father's. You are a true definition of a Proverbs 31 woman. Happy Mother's Day.

A warm thank you to all the mothers in the world. Mankind would be lost without you, and families would not be complete without your love, wisdom, and faithfulness. For all the working mothers having two full-time jobs, thank you for working so hard to help provide for your family, plus take on everything associated with being a mother. To all the single mothers who are responsible for both roles, may the Lord be your center of focus and strength. To all the men, be strong warriors, the mentor, friend, and spiritual leader to our families. Take a moment and look your princess in her eyes and show her how much you love her and the appreciation you have for your beauty on Mother's Day. What a powerful chapter, portraying a godly woman. This has personally opened my eyes and deepened my respect and honor for all the mothers in the world.

Lord Jesus,

Thank You for the entire population of mothers, living or who have passed on in this world, who you created for the specific purpose of being a mother. They have sacrificed their lives so families could experience life to the full. They stopped our bloody noses, sewed on lost buttons, and made sure our bellies were always full. I pray, Lord, you would bless them and reassure them they are exactly where You need them, because without them we would be walking around with bloody noses, wearing a coat without buttons, and have empty stomachs.

"Stand"

1 Samuel 12:16

*"Now then, **stand** still and see this great thing the LORD is about to do before your eyes!" – NIV*

2 Chronicles 20:17

*"You will not have to fight this battle. Take up your positions; **stand** firm and see the deliverance the LORD will give you, O Judah and Jerusalem. Do not be afraid; do not be discouraged. Go out to face them tomorrow, and the LORD will be with you.' " – NIV*

Standing shoulder to shoulder, weapons engaged, we prepared to take aim at our opponents standing 30 yards in front of us. We heard the command: "Prepare to volley, volley." Fifteen guns went off simultaneously and our paint balls struck our opponents, with heavy hits causing fatal wounds, according to the rules of the game. If a paintball hit the head or torso, it was considered a fatal wound, and if a limb was hit, it could not be used in the next round of fire. Several of our shots were right on target, including mine, striking the facemask of my now-dead opponent.

The fatally wounded fell out of the ranks and the remaining survivors prepared to fire back at us. My rank was kneeling on the ground while a second rank stood behind us. I quickly glanced to my left and right, watching my team stand with honor, preparing to take incoming paintballs traveling at 300 feet a second. I could see the excitement and uncertainty reflect on my team's faces, wondering if they would be fatally wounded. I have to say it was kind of scary, looking down the field at several barrels pointing in our direction, not knowing where their sights were aimed. The command was given: "Prepare to volley, volley.

Several guns went off at the same time. I closed my eyes, clenched my teeth, and prepared for the impact. I heard several paint balls hit my teammates and there were cries of pain as some took paint in the chest, abdomen, or head. You could hear the paintballs hit with a loud thumping noise. The mortally wounded, showing paint splats, welts, and broken skin from the precision shots, fell from the ranks. I did not sustain a wound, but do recall a paintball speeding past my left ear, just inches away from hitting me. Both surviving sides took one pace closer and prepared for the second round of fire. This continued until one side was completely destroyed. This was one of the team-building exercises used at a men's Wild at Heart retreat a couple weeks ago.

We will find ourselves standing in front of our enemy, the devil staring down the barrel of his gun. The enemy has his sights set on us and desires to destroy us using any tactic to remove us from the ranks. If we stand alone against the enemy, be prepared to be mortally wounded. But if we surround ourselves with other team members, there are more targets to aim at and a greater chance of survival. We will be faced with battles every day, and how we deal with the enemy will determine our success or failure. We must know where our strength is and how to use the power in the name of Jesus to send a bullet straight between the eyes of our enemy.

In times of battle, we need to form ranks shoulder-to-shoulder with our brothers and sisters in Christ, and stand with honor, integrity, and power. The enemy will try to fire his best shot, but the armor of God was designed to protect us on impact. Let the enemy have first volley, then we can prepare to fire back with the Word of the Lord, which will deliver a fatal blow and cause the enemy to flee from the battle. The important thing to remember is to continue to stand in battle until you defeat your enemy. We can rejoice because the victory is ours, given to us the moment Jesus Christ died on the cross for our sins. All we have to do is show up on the battlefield in the strength of the Lord, face our enemy with honor, and fire our best shot

Lord Jesus,

Thank You for giving us the victory over the devil through your death on the cross. I pray we would know the victory we have and use the power of Your name to defeat anything standing in our way. The Holy Spirit continues to remind us to don the armor of God daily as we prepare for a new day of battle. Let us show up on the battlefield not alone, and prepared to fight and stand our ground in honor of the Lord. Let us claim victory through the blood of Jesus, and boldly stand with no fear.

"I Will Not Forget You"

Hebrews 13:5-6

"For He God Himself has said, I will not in any way fail you nor give you up nor leave you without support. I will not, I will not, I will not in any degree leave you helpless nor forsake nor let you down (relax my hold on you)! {Assuredly not!} So we take comfort and are encouraged and confidently and boldly say, The Lord is my Helper; I will not be seized with alarm (I will not fear or dread or be terrified). What can man do to me?" – AMP

Memorial Day was yesterday, and the Lord laid a message on my heart. I wanted to share a true story about my second cousin, Brandon Zylstra. The story was written by Jessica Lowe of the *Newton Daily News*, called "Sully Man Awarded Silver Star for Heroic Acts in Iraq." Here is the story, paraphrased from my perspective, with a powerful ending.

On April 10th 2007, Brandon's platoon came under heavy enemy fire while traveling in a neighborhood of Baghdad. Rounds of fire came from different directions as they attempted to make a turn down a street with a loaded trailer of supplies for troops. Unable to make the turn, the platoon's caravan was halted, thus exposing them as sitting targets to the enemy. Brandon observed where most of the enemy fire was coming from and quickly devised a plan. He stood in the street under fire, preparing his platoon to engage the enemy.

A fellow soldier took an enemy round, and immediately Brandon rushed to his aid. Two other soldiers followed behind Brandon, providing cover fire. The four came under a barrage of heavy fire, wounding two more soldiers. Brandon had to decide who needed his attention the most and attended to the most critically wounded, dragging him across the street to safety. Rushing back across the street, weapons blazing in both hands, Brandon tended to the other wounded soldiers, risking his life, and was prepared to die for his fellow soldiers. Brandon's quick commands were able to divert enemy fire from the wounded soldiers and gave the platoon time to escape to safety.

Brandon continued to engage the enemy while clinging to a tow strap on one of the hoods of an escaping M1151 vehicle, after discovering no seats were left. His actions and quick thinking saved lives, and the most important thing to remember here is that he was not going to forget or leave one of his brothers behind. Brandon was awarded the Silver Star for his heroic act. One of his fellow soldiers said, "If it was not for Brandon, I would not be here today." We need to remember all the men and woman who have sacrificed their safety or given their lives for our freedom.

Do you know, we have someone who will never leave us nor forsake us once we are secured in the palm of His hand? The Lord desires all His creation to call upon the name of his Son, Jesus Christ, and secure a place with Him for eternity. God loves us so much, he sent His only Son to die for you and I. Jesus volunteered his life on the cross so we could live forever in freedom. The enemy desires the opposite, and wants to take us out with enemy fire. We have all fallen and been wounded with sin, and Jesus wants to rush to our aid and drag us to eternity, where the enemy can never touch us again.

Do you feel trapped, unable to escape, with enemy fire coming from all directions, and lying wounded from enemy fire? We have a Brandon who is willing to face the enemy head-on to secure us one by one. He will not stop, and desires all of His Father's children to be saved for eternity. He loves us all more than we could ever imagine, and will come to our rescue upon calling on His name. Once He has us in His grips, there is nothing that can take us away from Him. Jesus is on a mission to rescue the wounded and lost, and desires nothing more than to see all come to his Father through His sacrifice. Jesus wants us to say, "If it were not for Jesus, then I would not have eternal life today."

Lord Jesus,

Thank You for laying Your life down on the cross so we could have freedom. Thank you for continually being on a rescue mission, listening for our cries of help and rushing to our aid with saving grace. I pray we would realize we need to be rescued, and call on Your name, Jesus. Then we can know there is nothing to take us from the palm of Your Father's hand, and we can have freedom, joy, and peace from the battle.

"Get Excited"

Psalm 98:1 & 4

"O sing unto the Lord a new song; for He hath done marvelous things: His right hand, and His holy arm hath gotten Him the victory … Make a joyful noise unto the Lord, all the earth: make a loud noise, and rejoice, and sing praise." - KJV

Tossing and turning, staring wide-eyed at the ceiling, I could not sleep as the excitement was just too much for me to handle. All I could think about was getting up in a few hours for vacation. I could hear my mother rustling around the house, making the last preparations for the trip, and my father putting things in the car. This excitement had been building up inside of me ever since we started to count down the days on the calendar hanging in our kitchen.

My brother and I were going to Disney Land for the first time. We grew up watching the *Mickey Mouse Club* and other family Disney shows. I recall our family sitting down together, eating in the living room off TV trays, watching World of Disney movies like *Chitty Chitty Bang Bang, Herbie the Love Bug*, and *Mary Poppins.* Now we were actually going to this fantasy world to meet all our favorite pals; Mickey, Donald, Goofy, and Pluto. I was so excited, my heart was about to jump out of my body, and I was the first one in the car.

During our journey to California, my brother and I looked at all the pictures in the travel pamphlets my father had in the seat pocket in front of us. I remember how excited we both were, looking at pictures of the Pirates of the Caribbean, The Haunted House, and Cartoon Land. Our excitement increased and to rubbed off on our parents as they discussed some of the things they were excited to see again. Mom and Dad were like little kids, and the expressions on their faces indicated we were all going to have the time of our lives. The building excitement filled us all with joy as we sang songs most of the way there.

We need to get excited and make a joyful noise each morning we get up to spend time in the presence of the Lord. Nothing in our lives should be more important than the joy and excitement we have in walking with Jesus Christ. In **Strong's Dictionary,** the phrase, "Make a joyful noise," is defined as: "to split the ears with sound, shout for alarm or joy, blow an alarm." We need to be shouting at the top of our lungs, praising the Lord the moment we wake. We need to get excited and picture each time with the Lord as a long-anticipated vacation to our favorite destination. Excitement like that should wake us up early, without the need of an alarm clock.

We must make a quality decision right now to enjoy every day of our lives. It is our life, no one else's. We are the ones who make the decision to be ordinary or extraordinary for Christ. God is excited about every one of our lives, as He created each one of us for a specific purpose, so we need to get excited about that one fact. We cannot let anything or anyone steal our joy away from us, because no joy fills us with fear, worry, envy, and could lead to our destruction. When we know what our future holds in Christ, there is no room for anything negative.

If the devil has robbed us of our past joy, it is time to claim every minute back and know the Lord Jesus died at Calvary for a purpose, to bless us with joy, peace, love, health, prosperity, and more than we could ever think or imagine. So let's get excited every morning and expect great things to manifest in our lives. That new excitement will wake us up early, fill our hearts with song, and cause a new stride in our walk with the Lord. We need to let that excitement grow and affect us like the first trip we took to Disney Land. Instead of allowing disappointments to dominate our thoughts, we can spend quality time in the Word and saturate ourselves with messages of success.

Lord Jesus,

Thank You for being our joy, peace, love, grace, and fullness, lacking in nothing. It was Your death that gives us abundant life. I pray we would not allow anything to discourage, depress, or drive us away from You, because those are the enemy's tactics to draw us away from what You want us to ultimately have. I pray we would get excited about life, and know the bright and perfect future You have planned for each and every one of us. I pray we would claim back what the enemy has stolen from us, in the name of Jesus.

"Desert Journey"

Deuteronomy 2:7

"The Lord your God has blessed you in all the work of your hands. He has watched over your journey through the vast desert. These forty years the Lord your God has been with you, and you have not lacked anything." - NIV

I watched our enemies rapidly approach, crossing into the Red Sea, pursuing to destroy us. Moments from reaching the shore, our enemies disappeared before my very eyes as the Red Sea swallowed them up, like a tornado sweeping over the land, leaving total destruction in its path. We were free from the grip of slavery and the promise of a land full of milk and honey lay before us.

It seemed as if we were going nowhere, but Moses continued to tell us what the Lord had directed him to say. I recall him saying that day, "Do not be afraid, Stand firm and you will see the deliverance the Lord will bring you today. The Egyptians you see today you will never see again. The Lord will fight for you; you need only to be still." It was true. As I watched in amazement, the pillar of fire and clouds protected us from the enemy, and the aftermath was Egyptian bodies scattered across the shore.

Our journey in the desert was long and stretched over many years. There were many times when I was about to give up on Moses, but it seemed like everything he put his hand to was blessed by the Lord. I watch many miracles transpire right before my very eyes, like giving us all the meat we could eat, raining bread from heaven, bringing forth water from a rock, and delivering us from all our enemies standing in the path to the Promised Land. Moses continued to teach us the ways of the Lord, and through our victories and defeats, one thing remained true: the promise the Lord made to us through Moses would come to pass.

I look back over the long journey the Lord took me on, and see so many changes that had to be completed in me before reaching the Promised Land. It was a time of molding, shaping, and development of my character in the Lord. There were many time when fear, worry, and anxiety got the best of me, but the mercy, grace, and love of the Lord was much more powerful. The presence of the Lord never left me and always provided everything I needed. Moses continued to tell us our journey would not be easy, but would be rewarding if we would just obey and place our trust in the Lord. His last words were imbedded into my heart, as I watched all the promises come to pass when Joshua led us into the Promised Land.

Sometimes it seems we are wondering in the desert on a long, never-ending journey, and the only thing keeping us going is the promises we have in God's Word. There may be times when we feel like laying down and wasting away in the sands of death, giving up on everything. That is exactly what the enemy wants us to do; to never see the Promised Land the Lord has for us. There are reasons why we go through desert journeys; to mold us, shape us, develop us, and train us to be more effective for the Lord.

We cannot allow fear, worry, and anxiety get the best of us and keep us from entering the Promised Land. Instead, we must be still and latch onto the promises the Lord has given us in His Word. The Lord desires to bless everything we put our hands to, but in return, we must live in obedience to the Lord, putting Him first in everything. Let us look back on our journey and see the lighted path the Lord has taken us on, and see how He has provided everything we needed physically, emotionally, and spiritually. We must not give up on the Lord and forfeit the Promised Land He has for us. Instead, we must stay the course and claim what is ours.

Lord Jesus,

Thank You for giving us something we can place all our faith and trust on, Your perfect Word, given to us as a guide to life while we are on a desert journey to the Promised Land. I pray we would not get discouraged in a long journey, but instead see how You are shaping, molding, and preparing us for Your perfect plan. May we be encouraged by the truth in the Bible and know You are the same never-changing Lord, who desires only the best for His children.

"Defeated?"

John 10:28-29

"And I give unto them eternal life; and they shall never perish, neither shall any man pluck them out of my hand. My Father, which gave them me, is greater than all; and no man is able to pluck them out of my Father's hand." KJV

Lying face down in the cold, wet mud, exhausted, I watched through the corner of my eye as the opposite team's runner scored the winning touchdown. Thoughts raced through my mind, giving me a mental picture of a loser, slacker, failure, and worthless human being. I ran my heart out, trying to prevent him from scoring, but he was slightly faster than me.

There are times that I feel like I am face down in the mud of life, and the devil keeps whispering in my ear, "See? You are a loser, you have failed God, and you are worthless to the Kingdom." If we allow the devil to get a foothold on our minds, we will be convinced of those lies and soak in our defeat. The devil wants to hold us down in the mud until the game of life is over.

We are not losers, failures, or worthless! It is so easy to convince ourselves of these lies and become ineffective for God. Last night, I found myself questioning my purpose for the Kingdom and doubting that I will be used in the battle. Jesus Christ died so that we may have victory over the devil and all his demons. All we have to do is call on the name of Jesus and put on the armor of God daily.

So next time you find life, or whatever the circumstance, is holding you in defeat, claim the victory, shake off the devil, and pick up your cross. God is always with us and will never leave us. We were created for greatness, and the number one goal of the devil is to prevent us from completing what God has called us to do.

Lord Jesus,

Thank You for picking us up out of the mud when you hear us call. You are always listening for our cries, and You will never leave us nor forsake us. Your death on the cross gives us freedom over the devil. I pray we would gain strength in Your promises and know we are not losers, failures, or worthless. But that we are victorious through Your blood.

"Do Not Be Proud, But Be Afraid"

Romans 8:5

"For those who live according to the flesh set their minds on the things of the flesh, but those who live according to the Spirit set their minds on the things of the Spirit." - NIV

A 1973, lime green, wood-paneled hatchback Vega was my first car. I was so excited to finally drive, but soon became discouraged and wanted something more. No, I take that back … I wanted something better than everyone else. I did not appreciate what was given to me by my father, and attempted to modify the car to look and feel like something it was not designed to be, and still deep down inside I was not satisfied with what I had.

Months later, I convinced my father to take on a father-son project. We traded the Vega for a rusted out '66 Mustang. The Mustang needed a lot of work, and I did not realize the extent of the project until later, but all I could envision was the finished project: me driving to school in a cherry '66 Mustang. Several months, and several thousand dollars later the project was done! The '66 Mustang, blue with white racing stripes, new black interior, and fake centerline rims, was ready for show.

I was so proud of that car and washed it almost every day. All I could talk about was my new '66 Mustang, and I soon became obsessed over the car. I would boast to my friends and drive an extra lap around the school parking lot to flash the new paint job and shiny rims. Every Friday night, you would find my friends and me driving down Fremont Street in Las Vegas, advertising to the world. But deep down inside, I desired more.

One evening, returning from picking up a pizza for the family, I was involved in a serious car accident. I walked away with minor injuries, but the '66 Mustang was not so lucky. All my pride crushed beyond repair, I feared what my father would do once he found out. All that money and time we spent on this project, lost. My father raced to the scene of the accident, and the first thing he did was grab me in his arms and asked if I was okay. I replied, "Yes, Father, but the car —." He said, "Brian, it is only a car. You are much more important to me."

Like me, do you find yourself boasting or being proud of what you have, and at times being a model of envy? Do people want what you have? We were created in the image of God, and He does not believe in pride. The only thing we should be boasting about is our relationship with Jesus Christ and becoming a model of Him. Everything we are given is of God, but we need to fear Him, because what He gives He can also take away. The Lord will give us the desires of our hearts according to his will. We need to humble ourselves and be satisfied with what He gives us, and we need to stop trying to modify or change things in our own strength. It is our nature to always want more, and we will never be satisfied.

The Lord will allow us to boast and be proud for so long. Eventually, He will crush everything that is not according to His will, but He reassures us that we are the most important thing to Him and nothing else matters. I have been brought through one of these experiences recently, and believe me, it has been humbling. The Word of God gives us some advice on this, so we can stop being proud and boasting of the things of the world, and start boasting in the things that truly matter.

Lord Jesus,

Thank You that you are everything we need. Our hope, glory, and joy. Nothing in this world matters or compares to what we have in You. I pray we would see You as our number one priority in life, and not get caught up in the things of the world.

"Do the Next Best Thing"

Proverbs 3:3-7

"Trust in the LORD with all thine heart; and lean not unto thine own understanding. In all thy ways acknowledge him, and he will direct thy paths. Be not wise in thine own eyes: fear the LORD, and depart from evil." - KJV

"Should I go or should I stay?" This was the question I asked myself with my hand on the doorknob of my front door. I had just taken a hot shower, shaved, and dressed up to go out. It had been a few months after my divorce and loneliness had set in like rigor mortis. I was dying for attention, and got the wild idea a local bar could supply all my needs and eliminate the feeling of being alone. I must have stood at the door for what seem like eternity, then I asked myself a simple question.

"Brian, what is the next best thing to do?" This was a question posed to me by a close mentor and friend. Tom said, "Brian, any time you are unsure about what to do, think for a moment about what would be the next best thing to do to honor the Lord." It did not make a whole lot of sense at the time, but in times of uncertainty, it has gotten me through. A very simple principle, if applied, could make all the difference between glorifying the Lord or finding yourself in a situation not pleasing to the Lord. You are probably wondering what decision I made?

Of course, I did the next best thing and decided not to go out. Instead I brushed my teeth and went to bed. What did I miss out on by not going to the local bar? I am sure I could have had a great time and subdued my loneliness for a while, but in that state of mind, I might have compromised my integrity for a pretty face. I awoke to victory with Christ instead of a girl from the bar. There have been several times when I am faced with a situation, and immediately this comes to mind: "Do the next best thing, Brian." I have learned it helps in any given situation.

The Lord gives us the choice to decide right from wrong, and lets everything play through for His glory. Of course we have been given a guidebook on life, called the Bible. The more we read, meditate, and study the Bible, the better prepared we will be for any given situation. If our decisions are in line with what the Bible teaches, then we are safe to move in that direction, but if what we want contradicts the word of God, then we need to take our hands off the doorknob, brush our teeth and go to sleep.

The next time we find ourselves standing at the crossroads, we need to remember to ask ourselves a simple question: "What would be the next best thing to do?" It may sound crazy, but it really works. Trust me on this one. We have a choice to make and it can be right or wrong, but if we would take a moment and think it through, we have a better shot at making the right choice that honors the Lord Jesus Christ. We will all be held accountable for every decision we ever make in this temporary life, so why not make the best decisions from this day forward?

Lord Jesus,

Thank You for giving us your living word, used for teaching, rebuking, and training. Thank You that we can find the truth in your word and use it as a guide for our lives. I pray we would try and live by the example You give us through Your word, and seek the answers we are looking for in the Bible before making any decisions. Let us stop and ask ourselves: "What is the next best thing to do?"

"Tap Into The Power Within"

Acts 1:8

"But you will receive power when the Holy Spirit comes on you; and you will be my witnesses in Jerusalem, and in all Judea and Samaria, and to the ends of the earth." - NIV

O ur crew of six each grabbed a side of the raft and proceeded to the launch site. Approaching the site, I could hear the roaring water of the dam falling a hundred feet, crashing into the crevices of rocks below. We made our descent alongside the dam until we came to a small clearing, where we could launch our raft. My attention was drawn to the array of jagged rocks and the swiftly moving water all around us. I thought, "You've got to be kidding. We are going to launch in this?"

Our guide gave us specific instructions on how to launch from the site safely; however, he grabbed everyone's attention when he explained how the crushing water could kill us if we did not follow his exact commands. I had the mixed emotions of fear and excitement as we proceeded to check all our gear and cautiously enter the raging river. Placing one foot in the water, I could feel the current grabbing me, wanting to suck me in. I could see and hear how powerful the river was, but until I actually stepped into the river and felt its power, it was a totally different experience.

Managing to get into the raft, wedging our feet under the thick rubber seats for stability, gripping our paddles with death grips, we all watched the guide as he pushed us off the rocks and jumped into the back of the raft. Immediately, a loud command came echoing through the West Virginia valley, "Right side forward paddle, left side back paddle!" The rushing water was throwing us in different directions, the water crashing on all sides of the raft forcing us closer towards the rocks. Commands got louder, faster, and there was a since of urgency in the command as we prepared to drop into a deep hole.

I looked over my shoulder as I dug my paddle deep in the river. We started to fall sideways over a ledge of water, and the force of the fall caused one of our team members to fall out of the raft. I recall seeing his face full of fear as he was thrown into the raging rapids, then he disappeared. He was there for a moment, and then was gone as if the river swallowed him like a frog snatching a fly out of the air. The guide kept throwing commands at us, and shouted, "We will find him later, stay focused on me!" Now one man short, we continued to fight our way through the crashing, rock-filled water.

Several minutes later, we finally broke through and found some calm water. Hearts beating rapidly, adrenaline flowing through our veins, we all looked at each other with a sense of accomplishment and victory. Just then, we discovered our fallen team member wading towards the raft. We grabbed him from the water, dragging him back into the raft. He was exhausted from fighting the raging waters, and he stood up and showed us his battle wounds. His whole left thigh was red, bruised, and scraped from being thrown into the rocks. He explained it was like being sucked down the drain, then being shot from a cannon. I could only imagine the experience, but soon would get my opportunity.

Later that day, we had permission to get into the raging river and experience it for ourselves. Of course, this was a safe designated area for the activity. We were instructed to float on our backs, keeping our feet in front of us to push off of rocks. We also had to keep our helmets and life vests on, as we would be traveling downstream at a very rapid pace. One by one, we jumped from the raft into the river, and immediately the water grabbed us. I could not swim against the current or change my course in any way, I just had to surrender to the power of the river and trust where it was taking me. For a moment, fear set in, but eventually it passed and a feeling of joy came over me.

The rafting experience reminded me of the power we have in the Lord Jesus Christ. I am sure we have all heard about the powerful things Jesus did through the Holy Spirit, and have seen those miracles and wonders displayed in a movie about his life and ministry, but have we actually experienced the true power of the Holy Spirit that comes to live in us when we accept the Lord Jesus as our Savior? The power of the Spirit is more powerful than anything we can imagine, it was given to direct us, and we can receive joy and peace from it when we allow it to engulf us.

Do we truly realize the power we have in the name of Jesus? The power of the Holy Spirit is raging in us like a high flowing river, and all we have to do is jump in and trust the Spirit and not fear the power flowing through us to accomplish great things for Christ. There have been a few miracles that have transpired during my life, and it seemed as if I was being sucked in and shot out like a cannon, having no control, but the results were incredible. I just shake my head in doubt and cannot begin to understand what just happened through me. Can you relate to this power?

The Holy Spirit wants to accomplish great things through us, so let's tighten up our helmets, check our life vests, and jump in feet-first to experience the ride of our lives. The Holy Spirit wants to flow through us and use us to accomplish great things in the name of Jesus. If you want to experience this power, accept Jesus Christ and ask to be empowered with the Holy Spirit today. Christ said through the power of the Holy Spirit, we would be able to accomplish greater things in His name for the glory of the Lord.

Lord Jesus,

Thank You for sending us a helper and counselor to guide and direct us through the raging waters of life's experiences. I pray we would learn to trust the Holy Spirit that dwells in us, and to find joy from the power we have in Your name. I pray we would welcome the Spirit to use us, suck us in, and shoot us out, accomplishing great things for Your glory.

"Eyes of Jesus"

Ephesians 6:12

"For our struggle is not against flesh and blood, but against the rulers, against the authorities, against the powers of this dark world and against the spiritual forces of evil in the heavenly realms."
- NIV

The wrinkles on his face were deep and stretched, eyes like a dim light bulb, and through the crack of his smile there were a couple of teeth. As I approached, the stench of alcohol and body odor was strong. He had a couple layers of clothes on, and I noticed his pants were soiled with dirt and whatever else I could not imagine. He was missing one sock and both shoes looked like pieces of Swiss cheese.

He locked his eyes on mine but I quickly looked away and began to judge this man by his appearance. Thinking, " How could he let himself get like that?" I tried to avoid him altogether, but the Lord had a different plan. It seemed everywhere I went, he would show up in my shadow and I could feel him staring at me. At times, it was so intense I could feel his piercing stare penetrate my soul.

The church was serving the homeless with a hot meal that day, and I was asked to walk around and pray with people. I continued to avoid that man, hoping someone else would talk to him, but the Lord brought us face-to-face, and I found myself staring into his dimly lit eyes with nothing to say. Again, my mind was racing with judgmental thoughts towards this man when the Lord convicted me in my spirit and said to my heart, "I created him, he is perfect, and I have a perfect plan."

I tried to look past everything on the outside, but it was not easy for me because I still wanted to dwell on this man's circumstances and see him as less of a person. Jesus whispered softly in my ear, " Look at him through my eyes, Brian." My eyes immediately began to tear up and the lump in my throat was getting harder to swallow as I stood in front of this man, staring deep into his eyes. I saw a tear fall from his eye to match mine, rolling down our cheeks at the same time.

As Christians, we tend to focus on what we see and feel emotionally. We need to start seeing everyone as a perfect creation, created by the hands of God for a perfect purpose. Everyone included, the unlovable, the untouchable, and the lost. As Christians, we must remember God created every single individual on the face of this earth. He desires all His children to spend eternity with Him. We have to start staring at creation through the eyes of Jesus and not our own.

I desire to look past everything and see what Jesus sees in that individual. I know there is good in everyone, because the Lord put it in His creation. I would like to find that good and not focus so much on the bad. I think that is why I began to tear up that day, staring in those loving eyes as if I was looking right at Jesus dwelling in this man's soul. I am beginning to understand the second greatest command, to love your neighbor as you love yourself.

The next time that person cuts you off on the freeway, or offends you with a word, try not to judge, but instead love in response. Take a step back, take a deep breath, and look at the situation through the eyes of Jesus. Know our battle is with the devil and his demons and not with God's creation. As Christians, let's pray to break the bonds of the enemy on people, and to restore God's perfect plan for their lives.

Lord Jesus,

Thank You for your unconditional love, mercy, and grace. I know You only see the good in us and convict us with anything that does not belong in our hearts. Help us to see Your creation through Your loving eyes, and know our battle is not with the flesh but against the enemy having a foothold on Your creation in the Spirit. I pray we would step back before quickly judging, stare in people's eyes, and see why You created them.

"Get Quacky"

Psalm 149:3

"Let them praise his name with dancing and make music to him with tambourine and harp." - NIV

Five in the morning, half-asleep, I made my way to the studio. There waiting for me was Michael, and in his possession he had a large blue bag. We proceeded to studio B to prepare for my spot on television. I peered through the window to the studio and saw the show in progress, tons of equipment, and bright lights. I was getting excited and did not know what to expect. One of the TV anchors poked his head through the door and said, "You are on in fifteen minutes."

We unzipped the large blue bag, revealing a costume I was to wear on live TV. I proceeded to put the costume on with the help of an assistant. The orange tights went on first, and then the large orange feet followed. The large, round, yellow body was slipped over my head, fastened with a couple of suspenders holding everything in place. Finally the head of the costume was slipped on and fastened under my chin. I was ready to make my way to the live studio with my four associates.

The heat of the lights burned through the suit and beads of sweat formed on my brow. I did not care because the adrenaline pumped through my veins and the excitement was building. The production assistant gave us the thumbs up and we made our way in front of the cameras. Quacky the Duck and associates were going to get a little crazy early in the morning to promote a weekend event. We were introduced by the weatherman, Bob Herzog of our local Channel 12 News during the Dance Party Friday segment. The music started and we began to dance.

We all were jumping up and down, doing disco moves, and shaking our tail feathers, all in good fun for a great cause, supporting a local food bank. The excitement was building and we all lost total control and just went with it, no fear, no regrets. During the filming,

Christ asked me a question in my spirit: "Brian, how come you do not dance like that or show that much excitement about me?" When it was all over, I felt led to write this message and share these thoughts with you.

As Christians, we are called to worship and praise the Lord with all our hearts, minds, and souls. Then why is it so difficult for us to show the excitement we have for the Lord? When was the last time we jumped up and down, did a little crazy dance, or just raised our hands to the Lord? We need to realize there is nothing more important to promote then our personal relationships with a risen Savior. I bet Jesus dances for us, so why can't we return the gesture? So many of us praise and worship in private, but when it comes to stepping out in front of the lights live, we tend to hide our excitement for knowing Jesus Christ.

Lord Jesus,

Thank You for creating us to worship and praise You with every fiber of our bodies. Thank You for giving us excitement, joy, adrenaline, and just craziness. I pray we would use those to show You just how much we love You, and that we are not ashamed to step out in the spotlight and get a little crazy, promoting the greatest cause ever. Your death on the cross, Your burial, Your resurrection, and the fact You live in our hearts to the fullest. Holy Spirit, turn the heat up in our hearts and let our flames burn strong for the Lord.

"Hidden Princess"

Genesis 2:21-23

"So the LORD God caused the man to fall into a deep sleep; and while he was sleeping, he took one of the man's ribs and closed up the place with flesh. Then the LORD God made a woman from the rib he had taken out of the man, and he brought her to the man."
- NIV

Scrubbing, washing, sweeping, she did what she had to do, but knew in her heart she was created for something more. She felt beautiful inside, her heart was full of joy, and she whistled while she worked. Can you guess? A girl destined for greatness, a girl with a kind heart, a hidden princess named Cinderella.

Cinderella was a character wanting to be part of something grand, something important, something everlasting. She knew there was more to life, and wondered while doing chores what it would be like to be a princess. She yearned to be seen, desired to possess a beauty worth pursuing, worth fighting for. She wanted to unveil her beauty, and according to the fable, the fairy godmother assisted her in making her dream come true.

Eve was a hidden princess. Just read the story in Genesis Everything God created was beautiful, and Eve had to be breathtaking, just like the rest of his creation. Adam said, "This is now bone of my bones and flesh of my flesh; she shall be called 'woman,' for she was taken out of man." I imagine Adam's jaw hit the ground when he saw Eve reflecting everything good God created in those six days. God gave him his very best through creating a perfect, hidden princess from one of Adam's ribs.

All women were created to possess beauty inside and out. We should view each woman as a princess created by God. Do you realize Eve was created last, the final touch to the beautiful painting God created of the world? There are women screaming inside to be noticed, to be loved, sought after, and to be desired. They wait patiently for their prince to sweep them off their feet. Women dream of their prince dressed in shinning armor, fighting to rescue them.

Why do you think women love movies that reflect the theme of the boy saving the girl?

In the book **Wild at Heart**, by John Eldridge, John quotes, "Every man has to have an adventure to live, a battle to fight, and a beauty to rescue. A woman needs an adventure to share in, to be fought for, and to have her beauty acknowledged." Let me ask you a question: Men, when was the last time you rescued your beauty and let her know she is a princess? Women, when was the last time you let your man know that he was King of your world? Together, find an adventure that sets your hearts on fire with Jesus and live life to the fullest.

Lord Jesus,

Thank You for giving us Your best when you created the world. Your fingerprint is on everything, and we see Your beauty everywhere we look. Lord, I pray we would look at each other as the ultimate gift created by a perfect creator. I pray we would see one another through the creator's eyes and treat our fellow men and women as the princes and princesses they and we are.

"I Want it All"

Ecclesiastes 2:4-11

"I made me great works; I builded me houses; I planted me vineyards: I made me gardens and orchards, and I planted trees in them of all kinds of fruits: I made me pools of water, to water therewith the wood that bringeth forth trees. I got me servants and maidens, and had servants born in my house; also I had great possessions of great and small cattle above all that were in Jerusalem before me. I gathered me also silver and gold, and the peculiar treasure of kings and of the provinces: I gat me men singers and women singers, and the delights of the sons of men, as musical instruments, and that of all sorts. So I was great, and increased more than all that were before me in Jerusalem: also my wisdom remained with me. And whatsoever mine eyes desired I kept not from them, I withheld not my heart from any joy; for my heart rejoiced in all my labour: and this was my portion of all my labour. Then I looked on all the works that my hands had wrought, and on the labour that I laboured to do: and behold, all was vanity and vexation of spirit, and there was no profit under the sun."- KJV

Anxiously flipping through the Sears catalog, eyes scanning each page like an out-of-control copy machine, I was compiling my Christmas inventory to Santa Claus. There must have been hundreds of items to choose from, and I wanted them all. Had to have this and had to have that, oh, and had to have that for sure. I must have circled something on each page, and the final completed list handed to my parents was two pages long, front and back. My hopes were high that everything would be under the Christmas tree.

My parents reviewed the list as I attentively watched and reminded them not to forget item number 13 and 24. The next words coming from my father threw me in utter confusion: "Brian, you have a great list here, but you need to select your top three choices, and we will notify Santa." What, only three? What was a five-year-old to do? I wanted it all. Taking the list back, sitting down at the table, faced with the hardest decision in my life at the time, I had to select my favorite three items. I looked up at my mom and dad with those sad puppy dog brown eyes and said, "Can't Santa double my order?"

Why do we chase after things with an attitude of "I want it all"? The bigger house, nicer car, better job, and more stuff than we really need? The American dream is to have it all, and we are willing to go into debt to keep up with the Joneses next door. Why are we so consumed by the world? Could it be that we are bombarded with 3,000 advertising messages every day that promise, promote security, bring happiness, and ultimately convince us we need it have it to be someone? The funny thing is that everything we own now will be owned by someone else later, or someone can find most of our stuff in a Goodwill store. We can take nothing with us to heaven, no matter who we are.

There is nothing wrong with saving money and enjoying nice things, but how we relate to our stuff determines a lot about the course of our lives and how we'll respond to the relationship with us that God desires. Donella Meadows says it best, "People don't need enormous cars; they need respect. They don't need closets full of clothes; they need to feel attractive and they need excitement and variety and beauty. People don't need electronic entertainment; they need something worthwhile to do with their lives. People need identity, community, challenge, acknowledgement, love, joy. To try to fill these needs with material things is to set up an unquenchable appetite for false solutions to real and never-satisfied problems."

Jesus had it all, too, and was willing to give it all up for one reason. He had everything His heart desired, but chose to be born in a manger, wore one set of clothes, had no home, and gave His life freely so we could have it all. He only had to make one choice and gave up everything so we could spend eternity with Him forever. Jesus wanted and wants all of us, so the sacrifice He made was great. He was building His treasures in heaven and wanted nothing to do with the treasures on Earth. The Lord gives us money and talents to be used for the same reason. We need to be consumed with the Lord and not allow our stuff to consume us. The next time we find ourselves desiring or circling something we want in our minds, we need to ask ourselves a simple question: "Will this decision lead me to the freedom Christ desires for me, or keep me in bondage to the world?"

Lord Jesus,

Thank You for giving up everything, even your life, because You wanted it all. You wanted all of God's creation to spend eternity in heaven with You. I pray we would learn from Your example of how you lived while on Earth, and we would gain a new attitude to build our treasures in heaven and not on Earth. May we also learn from King Solomon that accumulating stuff only leads to bondage, and there is no freedom under the sun in the treasures built on Earth.

"I've Got Your Back"

1 John 5:4

"For whatsoever is born of God overcometh the world: and this is the victory that overcometh the world, even our faith. Who is he that overcometh the world, but he that believeth that Jesus is the Son of God." - KJV

Could you imagine being one of 300 soldiers assigned to fight thousands of the opposing force? Preparing for battle, thoughts racing through your mind, wondering if you will live or die on this coming day. I personally have served in the military, but never had the opportunity to fight for my country. I have total respect for those men who have dug their heels into foreign soil and fought and died for what they believed in.

Every time the Angel of the Lord spoke to Gideon, he said, "The Lord is with you, mighty warrior." But like me at times, Gideon questioned and tested God. God wants us to have faith and trust in all His ways. I personally have a hard time doing that, and find myself doing things under my own strength, only to be quickly defeated by the enemy. In the sixth chapter of Judges in the 14th verse, the Lord had to reassure Gideon that He had his back. "The Lord turned to him and said, 'Go in the strength you have and save Israel out of Midian's hand. Am I not sending you?'"

But Lord, Gideon asked, how can I save Israel? My clan is the weakest in Manasseh, and I am the least in my family. The Lord answered, " I will be with you, and you will strike down all the Midianites together." But Lord I am weak and I cannot do this. Do these excuses sound familiar? The Lord deals with us the same way He dealt with Gideon and his doubts. Christ wants us to trust Him with all areas of our lives, our finances, relationships, possessions, and know everything we have is a gift from Him. God wants to convince, possess, and use us for His glory.

What faith Gideon had, after God convinced him to fight for the Kingdom. How many times do we find ourselves testing God like Gideon did? Gideon said to God, "If you will save Israel by my hand as you have promised – look, I will place a wool fleece on the threshing floor. If there is dew only on the fleece and all the ground is dry, then I will know that you will save Israel by my hand, as you said." After several tests and an interpretation of a dream, Gideon finally had the confidence to take his 300 men and defeat the enemy. A great story in Judges that shows us the Lord has our back.

So, know Jesus Christ is calling us to be mighty warriors for his Kingdom. Do not be afraid to stand in battle for Him. He will arm you with the armor of God. The helmet of salvation, breastplate of righteousness, girdle of truth, sandals of peace, shield of faith, and sword of the Spirit. We do not have to test God; just know He always has our backs. So the next time we find ourselves standing before a massive opposing force, dig in our heels and understand that we have the victory through Jesus Christ.

Lord Jesus,

Thank You for giving us the tools for battle. Thank You that through Your death on the cross, we have victory over the enemy and do not have to test the Lord, because we know where our victory is in Christ. I pray we would be brave and not be afraid of battle, but instead would pick up our swords and boldly show up for battle, knowing the Lord Jesus Christ has our backs.

"Journey Home"

Matthew 7:13-14

"Enter through the narrow gate. For wide is the gate and broad is the road that leads to destruction, and many enter through it. But small is the gate and narrow the road that leads to life, and only a few find it." - NIV

W e arrived at our K.O.A campsite, and my brother and I were anxious to get out and explore. "Not until we get everything unpacked," my father exclaimed. I could smell the adventure lying just beyond the thick grove of trees. The bags were unpacked and my father had just finished driving the last tent stake into the ground. "OK boys, have fun and do not wonder off too far from camp." My father was very familiar with the territory, as we had camped there several times before. Those were the words we were waiting for and all you could see was the dust trail left behind us. We both raced into the thick woods to begin exploring!

We were caught up in the vastness of the woods, lost track of time, and soon found ourselves wondering aimlessly in different directions. "Mark, do you remember what path we take back to camp?" I asked. "I think we go this way" was his reply. "Are you sure Mark?" We were lost and panic set in, as it was beginning to get dark, even though we had only been away from the camp a short time. Then we heard a familiar voice crying out, "Brian and Mark, it is getting late, get back to camp. The adventure's over, come on back now!" We followed the familiar voice home.

There is a song entitled *Journey Home*, on one of the Vineyard worship CDs by Ninge Briggs that puts this in perspective. Here are the lyrics.

Sometimes I feel like I'm falling; Sometimes I feel higher than the stars; Sometimes I can hear you calling; Sometimes I feel lost but then I lift my eyes up, I see where I belong. Life is just a journey home, then I will be with you. Life is just a journey home. Sometimes I feel weighed down by this treasure when I think of all you've done just for me. Sometimes there's so much to discover; Sometimes I see the cost but when I lift my eyes up. I see where I belong. Life is just a journey home, then I will be with you. Life is just a journey home.

What are you journeying toward? Are you aimlessly wondering in the vastness of this world, lost, not knowing what path to take? Are you on the path of greed, the path of envy, the path of worry? There is a very narrow path that will lead us home to be with Jesus Christ that very few follow, and it is so easy to get sidetracked on a path leading us further away from camp and the safety of our father's arms.

Jesus Christ is waiting for all of His children to come to Him. In the busyness of the world, we have to stop what we are doing, look up, and listen for the calm, still voice calling us home. Life is a short journey to be with Jesus for eternity. He desires we stay on the narrow path and keep our eyes focused on Him, avoiding the wide path leading to nowhere. So if we are lost in the deep forest of life, stop and listen for the familiar voice of Jesus calling us within our hearts. Just know Jesus is searching for us and wants to save us. He is the only way to stay on the narrow path that will lead us home for eternity.

Lord Jesus,

Thank You that you loved us so much you sacrificed Your life so we could spend eternity with You forever. You desire we keep our eyes on You and stay focused on Your voice that speaks to us through the Holy Spirit. I pray we would not follow the path that leads to destruction, but would strive to stay on the narrow path leading us into Your safe arms.

"Kicked to the Curb"

2 Corinthians 5:18-19

"And all things are of God, who hath reconciled us to himself by Jesus Christ, and hath given us the ministry of reconciliation; to wit, that God was in Christ, reconciling the world unto himself, not imputing their trespasses unto them; and hath committed unto us the world of reconciliation." - NKJ

Drawn to my front door like two magnets of opposite polarity, peering through my small window in the door, I saw something that pulled on my heartstrings. It was just like one of those country songs coming to life. I was frozen at the door and did not realize how this would impact me after four years. I tried to hold down the lump in my throat, but with each glance the lump grew larger and it was getting harder to swallow.

I began weeping as I watched my ex-wife and her new boyfriend across the street, sitting on a love seat, and at their feet lay my ex-dog. I could not help noticing how they looked at each other as they snuggled and kissed. Every few moments, I would see my ex-dog glance toward my house, as if he knew I was watching. The way my wife was acting around her boyfriend reminded me of when we first met, five years ago.

My ex-wife moved across the street from me after breaking up with her boyfriend. At that time, I was prepared to reconcile if possible, but within a few short weeks she returned to his side and I felt kicked to the curb. This went on for several months, and many times I found myself back behind my door, watching my ex-wife, wondering if there was anything more I could have done to save our marriage.

Finally, the Lord revealed to me I had done my best by standing on the reconciliation line. Now it was time to get on with my life. I tried four different times to develop things again with my ex-wife, but it did not work out. I had to learn to forget about her and my dog. This was harder than I thought, as things would continually remind me through a song, place, or past thought. It is like taking two pieces of paper, putting glue on each of them, sticking them

Straight From God's Corner

together, and allowing them to dry. Once they dry, try to separate them. No matter how you do it, there will be parts of each paper still attached to the other.

The Lord Jesus reminded me through his Word that through His death on the cross, He reconciled Himself to mankind and He would never kick me to the curb. As humans, we are going to fail one another, and divorce is one of the most painful things you could go through. I prayed to the Lord for a year to move me or my ex-wife, so I could begin to forget everything about her and move on with my life. He moved her away. He continually reminds me of how much He loves me. It has been six years since my divorce, and I would not be who I am today unless I went through that desert experience.

If you are in a similar situation, I would caution you not to make quick decisions, or you may find yourself watching your ex with another partner. Make sure you do everything you can before pulling the plug, because once you pull the plug, that is when the desert experience begins. It may seem to be the best answer short-term, but take a moment and play the tape all the way forward and take a hard look at your future. I never thought I would see my ex-wife with another man, and I have to say it was the most painful thing I ever saw. I do not wish it upon anyone, because you do not want to experience it.

We may feel kicked to the curb at times or traded in for a newer model, but we have to remember no matter how bad things seem, there is one who is there to pick us up out of the gutter and send us in a new direction. Jesus Christ will be with us through everything, good and bad. The Lord is a character of reconciliation, and He desires to give us all a bright future. I know there was a reason for my desert experience, and I also know the Lord has a perfect plan for all of us. Do not allow the enemy to convince you otherwise. We have the promises of God, and He will never leave us nor forsake us.

Lord Jesus,

Thank You for loving us so much you died on a cross to reconcile us with the Father forever. All we have to do is accept your death and be reconciled with God. It is a wonderful feeling to know You will

253

never kick us to the curb and You are all about bringing the very best out in us. We may have to go through the desert, but You promise to be there every step and You will bring us to the other side. I pray we would not put our hope in the flesh, but would hope in the Spirit, knowing our lives are in Your hands.

"Life or Death?"

Galatians 2:20

"I have been crucified with Christ and I no longer live, but Christ lives in me. The life I live in the body, I live by faith in the Son of God, who loved me and gave himself for me." – NIV

Making my way past the crowd surrounding the keg, walking down a narrow, smoke-filled hallway, I entered a small room in the back of the house. The room was dark and everyone there looked like zombies who just rose from the dead. Some were lying back on the bed, staring at the ceiling, motionless. Others were gathered around in a circle, taking turns hitting the monster bong. The bong was a device used to smoke large quantities of pot or marijuana. It was a long cylinder tube open at one end and closed at the other, mounted on a base for stability. A bowl outside connected to a small pipe would extend down into the water at the bottom of the bong. Finally there was a vent hole in the bong to release the smoke that filled chamber, to be inhaled from the opening at the top.

This bong was tall, so you had to stand up to take a hit from it. They would load the bowl with a high grade pot called skunk weed, pour Jack Daniels over the ice and water in the bottom of the bong, light the bowl, and a volunteer would inhale, causing the water to bubble and filling the chamber with smoke. Releasing their thumb from the vent hole, forcing large amounts of smoke into their lungs, they would inhale as much as possible. The smoke would quickly expand in their lungs, causing them to gasp for clean air. The skunk weed was known to sneak up and bite you with a paralyzing high.

I was one of those volunteers who stepped up under peer pressure to take a bong hit. Wanting to fit in with the crowd, I compromised my integrity and went against everything my parents instructed me not to do, to partake in doing drugs and drinking alcohol. At first it was a couple of times here and there, but later it became a habit, and I found myself wrapped up in the lifestyle for many years, getting high, drinking when I could, and even dealing at times to support my habits. I was even arrested for stealing beer at the age of 18. I was knocking on death's door every time I decided to indulge in that activity. One thing pulled me away from death's door: I found the meaning of life through the saving grace of Jesus Christ at the age of 32.

The Lord wants us to experience life to the full. He did not create His children to venture down paths leading to their deaths. He did give us free will of choice and shows us right from wrong through His written Word. We must make the right choice...LIFE or death? The Lord revealed to me His definition of LIFE, found in Matthew 22:37-39: "Love the Lord your God with all your heart and with all your soul; and with all your mind.' This is the first and greatest commandment. And the second is like it: 'Love your neighbor as yourself.'" – NIV. Life is hinged on these simple verses and everything that goes against them will only lead to death.

We do not have to enter that smoky room and compromise our integrity due to peer pressure or wanting to fit in. We were created to be different and stand out like a sore thumb. It only takes one hit from a bong and we may find ourselves craving more and more, leading us down the wrong path. It only takes one decision to accept life through the saving grace of Jesus Christ, which will lead us down a path of abundant life. There is no other feeling greater than waking up each day full of the Spirit. Drugs and alcohol are only temporary solutions. Jesus is the ultimate solution. Choose life over death today, and discover the greatest high.

Lord Jesus,

Thank You for being the answer we are looking for. You are LIFE and through Your death we can have life abundantly. You defeated death at the cross, and through Your name we can break any hold the enemy has on us. I pray we would accept life over death, and know anything not representing Your two greatest commands will lead us to destruction. I pray we would see that it is never to late to find LIFE in JESUS and experience a high greater than drugs, alcohol, or anything of this world.

"Lifts Your Head"

1 John 1:9-10

"If we confess our sins, he is faithful and just and will forgive us our sins and purify us from all unrighteousness. If we claim we have not sinned, we make him out to be a liar and his word has no place in our lives."- NIV

My brother and I were very excited to help my father wash the car, as he promised we would enjoy some ice cream from Dairy Queen afterwards. My father was finishing his morning cup of coffee, reading the sports page, and chomping on the last bite of his donut. My brother became impatient, grabbed the keys to the car, and exited to the garage. He was determined to move the car out of the garage and begin washing it.

We heard the car's ignition turn over, and what followed caused our whole family to rush outside. Instead of hitting the brake while in reverse, my brother stepped on the gas pedal and accelerated down our driveway, coming to a screeching halt after he struck our camper with a large CRASH! I was the first one out of the house, and my father and mother quickly followed. I saw my brother sitting in the car at the bottom of the driveway, hands gripped on the steering wheel, and the look of shock glued to his face.

My father jumped over the hedge like a gazelle being chased by a lion and raced toward the car, my mother immediately grabbed the phone prepared to call 911, and I was thinking, "Boy, is he going to get it." I found pleasure in my brother's pain, as I was the one who always got in trouble, but today the tables had turned in my favor. I remained a short distance away from my father, standing in his shadow with my eyes glued on the developing situation.

My father glanced at the damaged camper and car. His face was blank of emotion, and he instructed my brother to get out of the car in a monotone voice. My brother slowly exited the damaged car with head hung low, eyes glued to the ground, and the same state of shock painted on his face. My father stood there in silence, looking down on my brother with his hands planted on his waist. Then he knelt down, took his large, calloused hand, placed it under my brother's chin and lifted up his lifeless head. Looking into my brother's eyes, my father asked, "Mark, are you okay?" and hugged him.

There will be times when we make quick decisions, not thinking, and find ourselves backed into a situation we do not want to be in. We find ourselves filled with shame, confusion, and fear as our heads hang lifeless, awaiting the results of our sinful actions. Why is it so easy for us to find pleasure in other people's pain, and quickly become thankful we are not in that situation? Can you relate? I was hoping to see my brother face punishment from my father for his actions, but instead witnessed extended grace, mercy, and love.

Our enemy, the devil, likes to point his finger at our sin and find pleasure in our pain. The lies he whispers in our ears tend to penetrate our souls and fill us with fear. We have Jesus, who desires to kneel down in front of us, taking His perfect, nail-pierced hand to lift our lifeless heads. He will look into our eyes and extend his grace, mercy, and love to us. If we confess our sin to Him, He will never remember it again, and will wash our soul clean with one drop of his redeemed blood. The next time we find ourselves buried in sin, full of fear, do not listen to the devil's lies, but instead confess our sin and receive God's mercy, grace, and abounding love.

Lord Jesus,

Thank You for loving us with Your abounding grace, mercy, and love. You are always there for us when we find ourselves buried in sin, waiting to lift our heads, look into our eyes and ask us, "Are you okay?" I pray we would not listen to the lies of the devil, and prevent fear, confusion, and shame from entering our hearts. But instead we would be quick to confess our sin and receive your forgiveness, knowing we are loved by Jesus Christ.

"Make It Happen"

Judges 18:9

"They answered, 'Come on, let's attack them! We have seen that the land is very good aren't you going to do something? Don't hesitate to go there and take it over.'" – NIV

The flag hanging in a tree was visible from a distance. Our team quickly gathered to strategize a plan before the whistle was blown to start the game. The plan was to send our two fastest guys to secure the flag before the opposing team could get to it. The rest of the team would spread out in a parameter and give cover fire. The game was paintball capture the flag, fifteen verses fifteen, with one identical goal: to get to the flag first and return back without sustaining hits.

The whistle sounded and our two men moved forward like an out-of-control forest fire toward the flag. A barrage of fire from the opposing team focused on the two moving targets. Paintballs hit everywhere, leaving splatters of florescent paint on the trees and the ground all around them. We watched them zigzag through the fire as our team advanced forward, responding with continuous fire to cover our brave warriors. One of the runners was taken out of the game when he was hit several times by the advancing team after slowing his pace. But our surviving runner did beat the other team to the flag and returned to home base, winning the game.

A famous astronaut named James Lovell states, "There are people who make things happen, there are people who watch things happen, and there are people who wonder what happened. To be successful, you need to be a person who makes things happen."

Are we Christians who make things happen, watch things happen, or wonder what is happening? The Lord desires us to make things happen through the strength of Christ Jesus. We have a choice to make, and personally, there have been too many times in my past of watching things happen or having nothing to do with things as I sit quietly on the sidelines. It is time to make a change in our priorities for the Kingdom, and step up to the front line, prepared to run.

It seems there are more people on the sidelines verses those in the trenches. The Lord desires we work together as a team and do our fair share. I wonder how may people wanted to attack the people possessing the Promised Land, and how many hesitated or had nothing to do with it. I bet there were a few shining stars, but the majority were burnt out with fear. The Lord was trying to give them something wonderful, yet they hesitated to possess it because there was something scary standing in their path.

How many times have we allowed something to stand in the path of a blessing, or allowed fear to prevent us possessing a land full of milk and honey? I will be the first to say 'me.' The Lord wants us to be like our two team members, fearless, and racing fast toward the goal. Yes, the enemy is going to try to take us out, but the faster we are moving in the strength of the Lord, the harder it will be for the enemy to take us out. There is a better chance of survival when we do not remain stagnant, and keep moving toward the flag. There have been times when we have allowed fear to freeze us from moving anywhere, and every time we are taken out by the enemy's fire.

Let's make things happen for the Lord. It is time to get off the bench and get into the game. We cannot be afraid to get hit or killed, and we must know where our true strength comes from. Remember who we are in Christ, and reflect on the promises He gives us in the Word. We can do, be, and have everything the Word of the Lord says we can have. We cannot allow the enemy to get us in their sights, and the only way is to keep moving forward in a rapid pace for the Lord. We can all be like an out-of-control forest fire, consuming everything in our paths, including anything the enemy sets in our way.

Lord Jesus,

Thank You for being our consuming fire, so hot the enemy is afraid to come near. You are our strength and shelter from the enemy, and we know You are always moving us in your strength and You have given us the victory through Your blood. I pray we would not be afraid to move in Your strength, and know who we are through the name of Jesus Christ. I pray we all would be the ones who make things happen, make a difference for the Kingdom, and never watch from the sidelines again.

"Most Prized Possession?"

Luke 9:23-25

Then Jesus said to them all, "If anyone would come after me, he must deny himself and take up his cross daily and follow me. For whoever wants to save his life will lose it, but whoever loses his life for me will find it. What good is it for a man to gain the whole world, and yet lose or forfeit his very self?" - NIV

Last night, being in a laughing mood, I decided to watch the movie *Ice Age.* It was about a prehistoric sloth, mammoth, and saber tooth tiger taking on an adventure of returning a baby to a family in an Eskimo tribe. Throughout the movie, there was a prehistoric chipmunk obsessed with an acorn. He was willing to risk everything to keep this one possession.

This chipmunk clings to this acorn like there was no tomorrow, or as if it were the last one existing on the face of the earth. There are several times he risks his life to keep it. He was almost killed by an avalanche, stepped on, struck by lightning, and frozen in cube of ice with the acorn just out of his reach. I found myself laughing hysterically, and drawn to the movie just to find out if the chipmunk keeps possession of the acorn. Then the Spirit of God spoke to me through this movie.

"Brian what are you chasing, and what are you holding onto that is more important than me?" Let me ask you the same question. "Do you find yourself chasing after things or holding onto things you see as more important than God?" Some of those things can be materialistic or self-centered actions. It is a proven fact that people see material possessions as more important, and they are willing to even risk their lives to keep them in their grasp. I heard a story about a man who requested to be buried in his Corvette, because he did not want anyone else to possess it. Others have been known to be buried with their possessions.

Do not get me wrong, the Lord wants us to have life abundantly, but he does not want us to place anything in our lives before our relationship with Him. He will give us the desires of our hearts, but we have to seek Him first and put no other gods before us. We get in trouble when the things we love take the place of God, and that is where we need to draw the line on our priorities. Let's take a moment and ask ourselves, "Is there anything in our lives interfering with our personal relationship with Christ?" If so, we need to get rid of them, because we cannot allow anything to be more important than the Lord. Let us focus on the things in heaven, not on the things of the world.

Lord Jesus,

Thank You for using a simple movie to administer a powerful point. It is so easy to get caught up in material possessions and find ourselves chasing after things that really do not matter. I pray we would take a moment to assess our priorities and rid ourselves of the things standing in the way of a perfect relationship with You. I pray we would change our focus to things in heaven and not the things of the world.

"One with Christ"

John 13:1

"It was just before the Passover Feast. Jesus knew that the time had come for him to leave this world and go to the Father. Having loved his own who were in the world, he now showed them the full extent of his love." - NIV

Sitting down for the Passover meal, everything was prepared and ready, I listened to the words of the Master. Every eye in the place was glued on our Teacher, and all ears were tuned to his every word. I had been with him now for three years, and during that time experienced many signs, wonders, and miracles. My Master had taught me many things and always challenged me to be more like him.

All the sudden, Jesus got up from his place and headed to another part of the room. I watched him take off his outer robe, fill a basin with water, and wrap a towel around his waist. He returned to the table and knelt down, removed my sandals, and prepared to wash my dirty feet. My first words from my mouth were, "Lord, are you going to wash my feet? He replied, "You do not realize now what I am doing, but later you will understand." "No Lord, you shall never wash my feet," was my quick reply. His response cut to my heart when he said, "Unless I wash you, you have no part of me." What was happening here? My Master and Teacher was doing the task of a servant? Gently washing my feet with his perfect hands, Jesus looked up into my eyes and reached for the towel around his waist to wipe my feet dry.

He proceeded to wash everyone's feet in the room. I could not believe what was happening before my very eyes. The same hands that healed the sick, raised the dead, made the blind see, and cast out demons were now washing feet? Every one of us was awestruck by this humble act of kindness. Taking the basin of muddy water, setting it aside, and putting on his outer garments again, Jesus returned to sit down at the table. His words ripped through the silence in the room when he asked, "Do you understand what I have done for you?"

We all looked at one another in confusion and tried to figure out the meaning behind this act.

Jesus spoke up, saying, "You call me "Teacher' and 'Lord,' and rightly so, for that is what I am. Now that I, your Lord and Teacher, have washed your feet, you also should wash one another's feet. I have set you an example that you should do as I have done for you. I tell you the truth, no servant is greater than his master, nor is a messenger greater than the one who sent him. Now that you know these things, you will be blessed if you do them."

Can you image Jesus kneeling down in front of you, looking up into your eyes, and washing your dirty feet? I personally think my reaction would have mirrored that of Peter. How could you allow your Teacher, Lord, and friend to take on the act of a servant, doing the lowly, dirty task of foot washing? How uncomfortable the disciples must have felt when this was happening to them, especially for Judas, who was to betray him only moments later. Do you understand the meaning behind this task, and how it applies to us today?

The Lord desires all of His creation to be equal. There is none greater or lesser in the Lord's eyes. We are supposed to see one another through his eyes, and that includes those who betray us. Do you mean you want me to wash other people's feet, to be a servant to them? Yes, we were all created equal and have one thing in common, whether we like it or not. We all were created by the same Creator. The world tends to segregate people by what they do, have, or the power they possess. Why is it so difficult to serve fellow mankind? Could it be our pride, ego, and will stand in the way of becoming the hands of Christ?

We need to break out of the mold the world has created, and begin to see everyone being equal through the eyes of Jesus Christ. I think if we would humble ourselves and become servants in love to one another, the world would be a better place. What a great example the Lord Jesus showed his disciples, and how the same principle applies to us today. Do you realize Jesus came to the earth to seek, serve, and save mankind? We are called to do the same thing He did, and through His name do even greater things. I want to challenge myself and you to take up a basin of water and wash your fellow man's and woman's feet, seeing them through a servant's eyes. Blessings will come through this simple act of love, as promised in the Word.

Lord Jesus,

Thank You for giving us an example to live by. Lord, Teacher, and Friend, you continually show us examples of a servant's heart, especially in the act of dying on the cross to take away the sins of mankind. I pray we would be challenged by Your examples and begin to serve one another with humble acts of kindness, and see all of Your creation as equal, not segregate people according to the world's standards.

"Opportunity of a Lifetime"

Ecclesiastes 5:10

"Whoever loves money never has money enough; whoever loves wealth is never satisfied with his income. This too is meaningless."
- NIV

The line at the register, consisting of a multitude of different personalities, seemed never-ending. Glancing around, I noticed a gentleman patiently waiting to purchase his lottery ticket who seemed dazed, as if he were daydreaming about something. Another women's facial expression portrayed great anticipation as she continued to scan over the numbers she had picked, and the two screaming children had no effect as her attention was drawn to the task at hand of securing the winning lotto ticket.

Thinking I had never had to wait this long to pay for gas before, I turned to the man behind me and said, "What is the big commotion about?" He replied, "Haven't you heard? The lottery is up to 142 million, and everybody wants to get in on it." I admit, for a moment, there was a temptation to place my dollar on the counter for an opportunity of a lifetime. I stared into space as I wondered what I would do with the money. Buy a new sports car, a huge house, or travel the world?

I think everyone is looking for that opportunity of a lifetime by winning the lottery, and there are those who are comfortable with what they have. Which category do we fall into? I will be the first to admit difficulty with this. I find myself envying what others have, and know in Proverbs 14:30, the Lord's word teaches that envy rots the bones. Jesus taught we should not store up treasures on earth, but store up for ourselves treasures in heaven. He said, "For where your treasure is, there your heart will be also."

Jesus also said, "No one can serve two masters. Either he will hate the one and love the other, or he will be devoted to the one and despise the other. You cannot serve both God and money." Jesus is urging us to invest our life in the Kingdom of God, and what I have failed to realize is that everything God gives us is His anyway. We have been placed in charge to manage what He gives us, and He wants us to bring glory to Him on the decisions we make with the resources given to us. I have to continually remind myself of the verse in Matthew 6:31-34

"So do not worry, saying, 'What shall we eat?' or 'What shall we drink?' or 'What shall we wear?' For the pagans run after all these things, and your heavenly Father knows that you need them. But seek first his Kingdom and his righteousness, and all these things will be given to you as well. Therefore do not worry about tomorrow, for tomorrow will worry about itself. Each day has enough trouble of its own." Do not get me wrong, the Lord wants to bless us with abundant life; however, we have to remember He can bless us with more or take away what we have, and that is dependent on how good a steward we are with what He gives us.

We have the opportunity of a lifetime, and God is ready to give it to us for the asking. God gives each of us everything we will need, and most of all he gives us the greatest gift of all, his Son, Jesus Christ. The good news is that we do not have to stand in line, wondering if we will get that break in life. All we have to do is ask Jesus to come into our lives. He will enter into our lives and bless us with more than money can buy. Jesus said, "Ask and it will be given to you; seek and you will find; knock and the door will be opened to you." So the next time we think about investing our money in earthly things, remember, God owns everything and we need to ask ourselves this question: "Is what we are doing furthering the Kingdom and bringing glory to God, or just putting more stuff in our garage?"

Lord Jesus,

Thank You for teaching us the simple truth that what lays in our hearts is where our treasure is. We know You desire our hearts to be full of You and the things of heaven. I pray we would see the opportunity of a lifetime as seeking the Kingdom first, and allowing You to give us everything rather than chasing after things that have no worth and only rust and fade away with time.

"Rooted and Grounded in Love"

Isaiah 61:11

"For as the earth bringeth fourth her bud, and as the garden causeth the things that are sown in it to spring fourth; so the Lord God will cause righteousness and praise to spring fourth before all the nations." - NIV

It has always amazed me how a small seed planted in a garden can produce something so good and nutritious for us. I remember my parents planting a garden in our backyard in Las Vegas, and still picture the harvest it produced. Each year, it seemed like the garden would produce an abundance of fresh vegetables for our family to enjoy. If the garden was maintained, it continued to produce, but if neglected, brought nothing of worth to eat.

It started with rock-hard ground having to be tilled and prepared for seeds. My father would work in the garden from early evening until dusk, cultivating and nurturing the garden. His blood and sweat went into the garden, and seeing the first signs of life breaking through the ground made it all worth it. Seeds tenderly planted sprang forth with life. Continued maintenance had to be poured into the garden, allowing a continued harvest of fresh vegetables for our family to enjoy.

There were times with adverse weather conditions had my father scrabbling as if he were on alert to protect life from sudden death. He did everything to maintain the balance of life in the garden, including erecting a scarecrow to ward off unwanted predators. There were many times when my father and mother worked in the garden together, removing unwanted weeds from the soil, taking the time to remove one by one until the garden had been restored to full productivity.

The same thing must take place in the garden of our hearts. Jesus starts with a hard heart, tilling and preparing it for the seed of the Holy Spirit. The moment we accept Christ into our lives, his Spirit enters into our hearts and will reside there forever, producing a new life to break through the hardness of our lives that came from being separated from the Lord. We have to be on alert always for the enemy, and nurture our hearts, continually careful not to let anything evil enter. We must pluck every weed from our hearts, restoring full productivity.

The two greatest commands we need to remember are to love our God with all our hearts, minds, and souls, and to love our neighbor as ourselves. We will find the love in our hearts to cause the love of Jesus to spring forth from us and nourish the lives around us. We will produce from our hearts what we plant in our hearts. So let's be careful to guard our hearts and honor God, Jesus, and the Holy Spirit with everything we do. Everything is based on love, and without love we have a dead garden.

Lord Jesus,

Thank You for giving us the gift of the Holy Spirit to reside in our hearts. I pray we would nurture what is in our hearts and allow the love of Jesus to shine through us to those around us. I pray we would guard our hearts, and may You be glorified with the harvest that springs forth from our actions, words, and thoughts.

"Need Help?"

Isaiah 65:2

"All day long I have held out my hands to an obstinate people, who walk in ways not good, pursuing their own imaginations." - NIV

Psalms 18:6

"In my distress I called to the Lord; I cried to my God for help. From his temple he heard my voice; my cry came before him, into his ears." - NIV

Eyes tightly closed, standing in one spot, I waited to be led to my starting point. It felt as if I were in a dark space that stretched into infinity. I didn't want to move, to prevent a collision with another individual or nearby tree. I was amazed how helpless I felt, simulating being blind, and having no sense of direction. It almost seemed like my hearing became fine-tuned to the slightest movement around me, like that of a bat.

I felt an arm grab me and lead me away from the rest of the group. It seemed like a mile, but in reality was a short distance to my starting point. My hands were guided to grasp a rope that stretched out in front of me. I started to explore my surroundings by running my hand as far as I could to my left and right without moving from my spot. A couple of feet away was a tree with the rope wrapped around it. The only security I could find at the time was my iron-clad grasp on the rope.

Several minutes passed, and eventually everybody was at their starting points. We were given the instructions to follow the rope around the course with our eyes closed, and try to get out of the maze. The command was given to start, so I began my blinded journey and quickly discovered the ropes went in all directions. I could hear several people trying to communicate their discoveries and give hints and directions. David said, "I think I am on the outside." Denny replied, "I think I am on the inside." Several times, I collided with other blind travelers, reaching around them to continue my quest for freedom.

A voice in the distance said, "If you need help, raise your hand." This seemed never-ending, and at times very frustrating, running into the same voices or familiar trees. I was determined to find my way out of the maze. Relying on my instincts, I found myself doing more circles in the dark. In frustration, I yelled, "Has anyone found the exit yet?" I could hear voices all around me and not one of them had the right answer. Then clear as day I heard, "If you need help, raise your hand." I had enough, so I surrendered and raised my hand. Quickly, a hand reached out and grabbed me, leading me out of the maze to freedom. There never was an exit to the maze, as the only way out was to ask for help.

As Christians, we tend to want to do everything in our own strength, and fear to ask for help. Well, that describes me at times, and this exercise our group did while attending the Wild at Heart retreat a couple weeks ago helped me understand a few things about life. There have been times in my life when it seems like I am wondering around in a maze, blind, confused, and having no sense of direction. Not needing any help, bound and determined, saying to myself, "I think this is the way I need to go." But eventually I'm worn out, stressed, and accomplish nothing.

The Lord God gave us free will to make decisions, but a decision made without God can be the beginning of a long, endless maze. Since that retreat, the Lord has taught me to not be afraid to ask for His help. It makes total sense to me now. Why waste time in a maze of fear and confusion when I can have the Lord direct me to where I need to be with His Spirit who lives in me? There was one problem with that, and that was having the patience to wait on the Lord. The "I want it now" mentality has always been my philosophy, but I am quickly discovering that leads me back to the endless maze. I have tried to change that thinking by raising my hand to the Lord each day, and saying, "I need help today, please direct my path for Your glory, Jesus." It has been a battle with patience, but it seems I am not so caught up in that maze of confusion, worry, envy, strife, and fear.

So the next time we find ourselves wondering in the dark, fearful, and trying to do something in our own strength, we need to listen for that still voice telling us, "If you need help, raise your hand." If we find ourselves overpowered with anything but peace, joy, love, mercy, and happiness, then we need to ask to be brought back into the light. We need to remember the Lord is one arm's length away, and is always ready to rescue anyone who asks for His help. It makes sense for us to raise our humble hands and ask for direction from our Creator who holds the map to our lives.

Lord Jesus,

Thank You for being there for us 24 hours a day, ready to step in and direct our path according to Your will for our lives. You desire for all of us to walk in the light and not in darkness. I pray we would learn to do things in Your timing, and not rush into the dark maze that only leads to exhaustion. Instead, we would humbly raise our hands to You and ask for Your will to be done, not ours, and wait on Your strong hand to lead us to freedom.

"See You on the Other Side?"

Luke 15:31

"'My son,' the father said, 'you are always with me, and everything I have is yours. But we had to celebrate and be glad, because this brother of yours was dead and is alive again; he was lost and is found.'" - NIV

Sitting on the plane, thumbing through the *Sky Mall* magazine, I thought how long it had been since I had seen some of my cousins and family. My mother always kept me well-informed of what has been transpiring in their lives, but to actually personally speak to them or see them face-to-face is another story. Some of my cousins have children who are married or preparing to get married. "Where has the time gone?" was the question I asked myself as I traveled to Iowa for a recent family reunion.

I was excited to go, but also felt somewhat alienated, since I have not taken personal interest in their lives. My family has always been very close, but it seems that is the only branch I climb on the family tree. I told myself I need to take more interest in those I love and care about, including distant family. At this reunion, there was family I had not seen for years, and to be honest, I had a hard time remembering some of my cousins' children's names. There has been distant family I have made more effort to stay in contact with, but on the opposite end of the coin, many contacts have been mainly surface relations or no relation at all until there was a scheduled family reunion.

Why is this? Am I too busy to invest time in their lives, or do I really care about them? Of course I do, but do my actions show it? I think about distant family on occasion, and of course I am always reminded by my mother, who is involved in all their lives to the last detail. After this past reunion, the Lord reminded me of the more important things in life. Loving your neighbor as you love yourself includes all family. The Lord also laid it upon my heart to make sure they all have knowledge of him, so we all can be reunited on the other side of this life in Heaven.

This also reminded me of the most important thing I have accomplished in my life to date. After becoming a born again Christian, the Lord gave me a mission to witness his love to my immediate family. The Christmas following my new birth in Christ, I visited in Las Vegas and convinced my parents and brother to watch the movie, *Jesus.* "The true meaning of Christmas" was my tag line. Four months, later I received a phone call from my sobbing mother, with the news of her and my father returning to church. Six months after that, I received a second phone call from my sobbing mother, telling me my brother just accepted Jesus Christ as his Lord and Savior. I recall a third time when my mother was sobbing again, after seeing her whole family in church together. I now know we all will see each other in eternity.

As Christians, we need to remember one thing and not get so caught up in self or our own personal walks with the Lord. There will come a time when everyone will take their last breath and pass from this world. The question we have to ask ourselves is: Will we see them on the other side, for eternity? If our friends and family are still living, then there is still time. We cannot afford to wait and no one is guaranteed to be here tomorrow. I have asked the Lord to help me bring more of His children back to Him. Would you join with me to make a strong effort to share the Love of Christ with others, and offer everyone the free gift of salvation? Everyone needs to be invited to the feast at the Lord's Table. None should be left behind without an invitation.

Lord Jesus,

You made it so we could have freedom in a personal relationship with You, by dying on the cross for all of mankind. Thank You for reminding me of the greatest thing I have accomplished in my life to date. I desire to tell as many people as I can about Your free gift to offer anyone who asks. I pray my fellow man would make a conscious effort to take interest in those around them, including close friends and family, and boldly tell them about You before it is too late. I know God desires to see all the faces of His children on that final Day of Judgment.

"Hidden in the Closet"

1 John 1:9

"If we confess our sins, he is faithful and just and willing to forgive us our sins and purify us from all unrighteousness." - NIV

Mom asked, "Did you clean your room, Brian?" I responded with a quick nod of my head and tried to retreat out of the room as quickly as possible. She responded, "Hold on a minute. We will just have to take a look for ourselves, won't we?" I stopped dead in my tracks, fear setting in, and we proceeded back to my room. I had hoped an important phone call would distract her, or one of her friends would come over for a visit, but had no such luck.

At first glance, my room looked immaculate, and you would never know what lurked under my bed or what was stuffed in my closet. I thought the appearance of a clean room would buy me time to play with my friends, then clean it up later. That hypothesis failed when she kneeled down by my bed and glanced under it. She looked at me and said, "Clean room, huh? I wonder what else I can find." I thought, "Not the closet, please not the closet!" But her next stop was my closet, and she was not happy to discover the whole contents of my room crammed inside.

Needless to say, I never did have the opportunity to play with my friends that afternoon. Instead, I was restricted to my room for most of the day. I tried to cover up my mess with lies, and it only led to bigger problems. Taking the time to clean my room in the first place would have prevented me from lying to my mother and allevi-ated me from facing the consequence of my actions. I was willing to avoid confrontation by lying to my mother, and to this day I battle with the same issue.

Several months after my divorce, I had to face something in my life that had been hidden in my closet for years. I have been living behind an image that has gotten the best of me. I was successful, had my life in order, and was a devoted Christian. What I was hiding was my fear of confrontation. I was a compulsive liar and avoided all forms of confrontation like the plague. Through circumstances, the Lord showed me what has been hiding in my closet and called me to clean it up. He continues to reveal to me the messes I have hidden away, and shows me His truth that wipes everything clean.

The process with confrontation took months to overcome, but today that fear has been swept away from my closet forever. There are other things he is dealing with in my life, but slowly my closet is becoming less cluttered and more organized. "What are we hiding under our beds or what are we hiding in closets?" Everything we hide will eventually be discovered, and the sooner we clean up our room, the less consequence we will have to face. It never pays to hide things from God, because he can see everything we are hiding. It makes sense to come clean with the Lord and allow Him to reveal to us the truth that can set us free from our own dirty room of a conscience. What would Jesus see today if he looked under our beds or in our closets? What fears are lurking there, what sin is tucked under a dirty shirt, or what lies have you rationalizing between right and wrong?

Lord Jesus,

Thank You for being the truth that can set us free. You know all things, even the things we keep hidden under our beds or in our closets. I pray our conscience would get the best of us, and we would come clean with You, Lord, revealing everything so there is nothing hidden from You, so we could live free and know our hearts are clean and holy, giving You all the glory.

"The Power of the Heart"

Colossians 1:11

"Being strengthened with all power according to his glorious might so that you may have great endurance and patience, and joyfully."- NIV

Taking up the hobby of boxing has been a new adventure for me, used to eliminate the fear of confrontation and fighting. Running, hiding, and fear have been a big part of my life for several years, and they are being replaced with strength, honor, and bravery. I have learned there is no hiding in boxing, as it is a one-on-one sport and everything is exposed, both strength and weakness.

Understanding the concept of the sport and finding my heart through boxing has been difficult, but after my last session, that perspective has changed. As my boxing partner, Tom, stated, "You have to find your heart, Brian. It takes heart to overcome adversity. Once you find your heart, you can overcome anything in life!" A true example of this was working with the speed bag. If you are not aware of what a speed bag is, it is a small leather bag that hangs from a backboard, and the object is to bounce the bag off the backboard after hitting it with your hand in a repetitive manner.

Facing this obstacle, I thought it would never be possible to hit that bag every third count, and for the longest time it was taking me every sixth count or more to hit the bag on a semi-continuous basis. This was a very frustrating process, spanning the past several weeks. I have had a few choice words with that speed bag, but the final result of not giving up and devoting all my heart to this task has been very rewarding. My partner, Tom, told me that God was using the sport of boxing to strengthen and develop my heart, and I am beginning to understand this process.

I am beginning to understand how David stood against the giant, Goliath, with a sling and stone, while thousands of soldiers and a king observed. David put all his heart into it and trusted God with the results. Standing against a nine-foot giant took heart and guts.

The heart is where David found his strength to overcome the adversary that stood before him. It takes a lot of faith to stand up to adversity, as it is easier to be passive and let fear crush us. What giant is standing in our paths? It maybe as small as a boxing speed bag, or as large as a Goliath, but a strong heart can bring victory and crush those mountains standing in our way.

Jesus taught that we will face adversity in our lives. The decision we make on how to handle any given situation is what truly matters to the Lord. God will test our hearts and strengthen our faith through tests and trials. Don't let the giant standing in our paths detour us from moving forward in power. Let's ask God to help us find our hearts, and then use his strength in our hearts to defeat anything opposing us. The mind is the weakest link, so do not allow the enemy to convince us of defeat. Instead, let our hearts be filled with God's power, and know we can be victorious in the power that resides in us.

Lord Jesus,

Thank you for giving us the Holy Spirit that dwells in the hearts of your children in power. You said we can do all things through Christ who strengthens us. I pray we would not allow the enemy to convince us we are weak and worthless, but instead we can boldly stand before the giants in our lives with no fear, knowing You will deliver them into our hands in victory.

"Straight as an Arrow"

Isaiah 48:17

"This is what the Lord says, your redeemer, the Holy One of Israel: I am the Lord your God, who teaches you what is best for you; who directs you in the way you should go." - NIV

Grabbing my bowling shoes, sizing up my ball, I proceeded to lane 35. I was grouped with four other bowlers and my name was placed second on the monitor. It had been a year since bowling last, and I recall my scores being the lowest of all players. I entered into this night of bowling with an open mind and gave my fellow bowlers an advance warning of my bowling skills. All our names were registered, balls were placed in the holding bend, and we were ready to bowl.

The first bowler secured his ball and made his way to the deck. I watch him as he sent a 17-mile-an-hour ball down the lane, striking nine of the ten pins, then his second ball easily picked up the spare. What a tough act to follow, as I picked up my 15-pound ball and made my way to the deck. I stood there a moment, assessing my strategy of attaining a strike on my first swing of the ball. I took three cautious steps toward the foul line, eyes focused on the pins at the end of the lane. I let go of the ball and watched as it made its way down the lane striking only one pin after bouncing out of the gutter. It was going to be a long night of bowling, I thought.

I tried to hide the disappointment on my face as I returned to my seat, but it was a dead give away to my team members. One placed his hand on my shoulder and said, "You will get a strike next time." His words went in one ear and out the other as I thought, "Yeah, right." We had a bowler on our team who averaged close to 200 points per game, and two times in his past had bowled a perfect game of 300. My eyes were glued to his every move as he gracefully released his ball, and I watched it float down the lane, curving from one side to the other, striking the sweet spot, and sending all ten pins crashing to the ground. Strike!

I waited a few minutes, then pulled him aside, asking for a couple of tips. He told me not to look at the pins but to focus on the arrows on the lane, and release the ball with a stiff, straight arm. He watched my gutter roll and educated me on my arm crossing my body at release, explaining the attraction to the gutter. My name appeared on the monitor and it was time to bowl again. I stood on the deck, frozen with doubt. Moments had passed, and my teammate urged me on to throw the ball and to remember everything he told me. Taking my eyes off the pins, focused on the arrow in the center of the lane, I allowed my arm to brush my side, releasing the ball. I noticed my ball was going exactly where the arrow directed, and within moments I had a strike to add to my score.

There have been times when I take my eyes off Jesus and I find myself bouncing out of control instead of being on course. I tend to look down the lane of life and focus on the issue that stands before me, instead of relying on the arrow to direct me towards the sweet spot, sending everything crashing to the ground. We can easily become frozen with doubt and allow fear to enter our minds, telling us we are only going to wind up in the gutter of life again. If we continue to believe those lies, then we will always find ourselves attracted to the gutter, walking back to our seats full of disappointment.

We need to take our eyes off whatever is standing at the end of the lane and place them on Jesus, who will make our path straight, directing us towards victory. Then we must confidently throw our ball with a straight, stiff arm, knowing Jesus is our arrow to line up with. We can lift our eyes in confidence, knowing Jesus is in control of our lives according to His will. The formula to get a strike in life is to take our eyes off the end result, focus on lining up with Jesus, and trusting the arrow to lead us to victory.

Lord Jesus,

Thank You for being our light in darkness, for loving us so much by going to the cross for our sins, and giving us a straight path to your Father in Heaven. I pray we would take our eyes off what is at the end of our lane and focus on You, the arrow that can send us to the strike zone. I pray we would see You as our only source of victory when we are faced with any situation, and surrender everything to You, allowing You to direct our paths.

"The Good News"

Mark 1:15

"The time has come," he said, "The kingdom of God is near. Repent and believe the good news!" – NIV

Logging onto the Internet or turning on the TV, I am hit immediately with the news. In all of my life, I have never heard or seen so much negative news, and yes, I can choose to allow it to affect me or not. I have asked myself the question, "Why do people cling to bad news?" I was recently on a business trip and over breakfast I heard a table gossiping about how terrible everything was and how our futures looked bleak. I almost found it entertaining to hear just how much negative gossip was generated through the media, and how it affected these people sitting a couple tables away. Believe me, I tried to disengage from listening, but some of the things said almost had me convinced of the lies, too.

Over the past few weeks, I have noticed more people allowing fear to drive them, and it seems every conversation eventually turns toward the negative news surrounding us. Just last week, I found myself making a phone call to my financial planner in concern for the future of my 401K. Again, a couple nights ago, after turning on the TV, I was quickly absorbed with the headline news and began to allow fear to enter my spirit. I had only watched a few minutes of the news and quickly found myself worried, depressed, and fearful. It got so bad I had to turn off the TV, and I quickly picked up my Bible to read the promises made to me through the Lord's Word.

As Christians, we need to stop feeding on all the negative news in the world and start claiming the best news. There is only one headline we should be proclaiming, and that is "Christ Lives!" That news overpowers any negative news we may be facing today, and we are commanded to share the good news with anyone who will listen. I personally feel this is the best time to share the good news of Jesus, as a comeback to anything negative we hear from the people around us. We may hear, "I just do not know what I am going to do to survive." We can respond with words from Paul, "God will meet all your needs according to his glorious riches in Jesus Christ."

The Lord has spoken to my spirit recently and said, "Brian, it is time you stop just warming a pew and start impacting the Kingdom each day I bless you with." I asked myself, "How am I impacting the Kingdom every day for Jesus?" So I have decided to make some changes, disconnect from everything negative going on, and start sharing the most positive news of all time. I know time is short in this life, but we are not supposed to be focused on the things of the world, but on the things we cannot see, and build treasures in Heaven.

I have decided not to accept any bad news to enter my spirit, and to stay connected to the source that has overcome the world by shedding his precious blood on the cross, so all of mankind can spend eternity with God. If I have to unplug my TV set, limit what I watch on the Internet, or just boldly counter people's negative news with the good news of Jesus, then I am willing. If we only allow good things in, then good things will come out, but if we allow bad things in, then bad things will come out. The choice is ours to make, and this is the perfect time to make a difference, one life at a time.

We cannot allow fear, worry, or anxiety to pin us down. We must make an impact for Jesus Christ. Things seem to get worse every day, but one thing will never change no matter how bad things get. Jesus Christ loves us all, and He personally died for us so we could have freedom and no one, not even the devil, can take that from us. It is time to stand up and impact the people around us for Jesus. We do not need to cram the Gospel down people's throats, but simply make an effort to share what is living in our hearts, and there is no room for negative headlines there.

Lord Jesus,

Thank You for being the good news. The news told about Your death on the cross, being buried for three days, and rising from the grave to live in the heart of anyone who calls on Your name. The good news all of mankind needs to hear and then choose to spend eternity with You or without You. I pray all of creation would choose to not listen to all the negative headlines and lies, but instead would focus on one headline, "Christ Lives!" and then boldly proclaim Christ living in and through them, sharing the greatest news of all time with those around them.

"The Perfect Team"

Ephesians 6:10-11

"Finally, be strong in the Lord and in his mighty power. Put on the full armor of God so that you can take your stand against the devil's schemes." – NIV

Hebrews 4:12

"For the Word of God is living and active. Sharper than any double-edged sword, it penetrates even to dividing soul and spirit, joints and marrow; it judges the thoughts and attitudes of the heart." - NIV

Putting its head down in a bobbing fashion, tramping his front left hoof on the ground several times, the horse made the turn to face the waiting opponent. The knight sitting upon his back gave the signal, and as a team they proceeded into battle. The horse and rider rode toward the opposing team at full speed like a runaway train. Both horse and knight had to do the job they were trained to do in order to claim victory over defeat. There was a fifty percent chance, and their fate would soon be decided.

The two horses ran straight toward one another with no fear, only determination in their eyes. The knights both stretched out their lances toward one another, aiming for the perfect blow. The horses looked as if they were breathing fire, with their manes and tails blowing in the wind. The knights leaned forward, cradling their lances and zeroing in on each other. Within minutes, the horses were a lance apart, and the inevitable happened. First there was a loud crash when their lances made impact as the horses passed one another, then a shower of splintered wood and debris flew onto the battlefield, and finally you could judge the result by the reactions of the riders. In this case, the opposite rider was impacted so hard it forced him off the back of his horse, thus giving victory to our knight.

Yesterday, some close friends and I had the opportunity to experience this firsthand at the Ohio Renaissance Festival. This is a yearly event where, for a period of weeks, a series of people reenact the Renaissance period, allowing us visitors to step back in time for a realistic presentation. These actors and actresses have been doing this for years and it shows. I do not know how many hours of practice it takes to pull off the show and make it look so real, yet keep it safe. Experiencing this festival, I felt as if I was in those times, and

I could do what they did. "Okay, I am ready. Suit me up and put me on the back of that horse. I am ready ... let's rock!"

As Christians, we tend to get the idea we can face our enemy with no training at all. We must realize our enemy has been through extensive training, and the only thing on their mind is to destroy us and knock us off our horse. There have been so many times we find ourselves lying on our backs, wondering what just hit us. Each time we wake in the morning, we must suit up with the armor of God, but we also must ride a trained horse and practice and practice together as a team before beginning to think about riding into battle against the black knight.

The Word of the Lord is our partner, and the armor we wear will not complete the task alone. Both have to work together in the power of the Holy Spirit. We have to stay in the Word and train in it every day. The Word of God is like a focused, confident horse carrying its rider to victory over the enemy, head-on. We as riders need to trust in the armor we wear and focus, placing our lance dead on our enemy's heart. We can ride past our enemy, trusting the blow will leave them lying flat on their backs, wondering what just hit them. Using the armor of God combined with the power of the Lord's Word, we can ride into battle and know victory is ours for the taking.

Lord Jesus,

Thank You for the power of Your Words and for the Armor of God designed to protect us from the fiery darts or anything the enemy tries to throw at us. I know the enemy rides every day, and his lance is aimed at our hearts, wanting to destroy us. I pray we would take this seriously and stay in Your Word day and night, practicing for the battles to come. I pray we would wake each morning and suit up in the armor of God, then use the power of your Word to defeat our enemy.

"Crouching Sin"

Genesis 4:6-7

"Then the Lord said to Cain, 'Why are you angry? Why is your face downcast? If you do what is right, will you not be accepted? But if you do not do what is right, sin is crouching at your door; it desires to have you, but you must master it.'" - NIV

Her eyes locked onto mine as I pushed the limits with my mother and stared back with determination. "Don't you dare do that Brian!" she exclaimed. I continued to provoke her with my actions at the dinner table. Again she said, "You better not do that or you will suffer the consequences of your actions, young man!" My pride was strong like an unbroken horse, my rebellious nature overtook me, and I threw the spoon full of mashed potatoes across the room.

After the act, glancing at my mother, I began to laugh and point at the sculpture of potatoes on the wall. My mother's face turned a shade of red. Clenching her jaw, she mumbled through her teeth, "Now you did it, young man!" My laughing quickly came to a screeching stop, and instantly knew I was in trouble. Some say it was terrible twos, others would say I was just exploring my boundaries, but now I look back on the event and it was deliberate disobedience towards my mother. Needless to say my rear end eventually matched the shade of her face.

I did learn a valuable lesson, and as a result did not throw my food again. My mother was serious, and she had given me several warnings, but it was in my nature to push the limits and see what the end result would be. It all started in a thought, wondering what type of sculpture could be created on the wall. That thought quickly developed into an action as I scooped up a large portion of potatoes, and cocked my arm back to throw. Finally, I was past the point of no return, refusing to heed the warnings, and went through with the plan. Once the act was completed, it was no longer a game or funny, and I had to answer for my actions.

It is so easy to fall to sinful desires that can bring serious consequences if we act on them. It all starts with a thought and quickly can fester into sinful action if we allow it. *If we allow it* is the key thing to remember. The decision we make is either to turn and run from sin or allow it to get a foothold on us. Those who have a personal relationship with Jesus have a weapon living in their hearts called the Holy Spirit, who was sent by Christ to help us in these battles. I will be the first to admit my weakness in the flesh, and cannot count the number of times I have decided to act on things, leading to a big mess on the wall.

The next time we find ourselves holding a spoonful of mashed potatoes, with our arms cocked back ready to throw, let's stop and ask ourselves a simple question. "Is what I am about to do going to bring honor to the Lord, or will it draw me away from the Lord?" When sin is crouching at our doors, it desires to overtake us, but we are the ones who give sin power. We must master sin with the power of Jesus living inside us. The Scripture does not say 'learn to master' or 'try to master,' it says we 'must master.' If we do not master the sin in our lives, the results will be more costly than a red rear end.

Lord Jesus,

Thank You for sending the Holy Spirit to help us with our battles. I pray we would take Your Word seriously and know we must master the sin in our lives with Your power, not ours. I pray we would ask the simple question, "Are my actions, words, or thoughts bringing honor to the Lord?" Holy Spirit, make us sensitive to the alarm telling us not to continue that thought or action, and let us claim victory over sin through the blood of Jesus!

"Thief in the Night"

John 10:10

"The thief comes only in order to steal, kill, and destroy. I came that they may have and enjoy life, and have it in abundance (to the full 'til it overflows)." - AMP

"Women and children first," a cry in the cold, motionless night from the crew echoed over the decks. Rumors began to multiply quickly among the assembling passengers: Did we lose a propeller? Why have we stopped? Did we strike an iceberg? Why were we instructed to wear our life vest? This was a ship labeled as being indestructible and unsinkable upon its completion in 1912. Some of the most prominent people stepped aboard this ship with great enthusiasm and expectations, not knowing this man-made ship would lead them to their fate.

Earlier today, I had the opportunity to tour the *Titanic* exhibit at the Cincinnati Museum Center. I was handed a boarding pass of a first class passenger by the name of Mr. Charles Duane Williams. He was an actual passenger whose fate rested in the hands of the *Titanic*, as he was one of the 113 first class passengers who did not survive the night. He and his son Ron were traveling from Geneva, Switzerland to Pennsylvania, where his wife Lydia Biddle Williams-White awaited their arrival, never to see them again.

Walking down the hallway of the reconstructed first class cabin quarters, I tried to imagine what it would have been like to be Charles Williams. The beauty inside was breathtaking, the suites were never-ending, and the expense was insurmountable. It had to be one of the most exciting days of his life to experience stepping aboard the Titanic. Money was no option; only the best for first class, choice meals on custom dishes inlaid with gold; the finest champagne and brandy to harmonize with the premium cigars. It was paradise away from land, but he had no idea what would transpire in the next few hours of April 11, 1912.

They say it sounded like fingernails dug into a chalkboard, but a hundred times louder. Some of the first class passengers observed an immense iceberg through their suites' porthole windows. The first class deck was elevated above where the iceberg had ripped into the hull, flooding the lower decks. What was Charles Williams thinking while sipping his warm brandy and puffing on that choice cigar? I question what was going through his mind, observing everyone grabbing for their life vests and seeing fear illuminate in passengers' faces. I wonder how he felt after being asked to head in the direction of the lifeboats. I should think, like everyone else standing in disbelief, he deliberated with himself that this couldn't be happening to a ship claiming to be unsinkable, but reality painted a different picture.

Towards the end of the exhibit, I walked into a room, cold, gloomy, and voiceless. The collected pictures and artifacts sent chills down my back and put a lump in my throat. The *Titanic* lay motionless two-and-a-half miles below the ocean's surface. The debris field stretched for miles, a graveyard containing the innards of the *Titanic.* Death lying on the ocean floor was all I could visualize, hundreds of lost souls never seeing the light of day again, one of them being Charles Williams. He had no idea this would be the last time he would see his son or his wife. Like a thief in the night, death crept in and claimed his life, sending him to an icy grave.

We will never know when our time will come to meet our maker. It will come like a thief in the night. We can't run from death, and eventually death will stare us in the face. We have no guarantee of tomorrow, and we may be stepping aboard a *Titanic*, not knowing the fate that awaits us. Make sure we kiss, hug, and say, "I love you" to our loved ones, because we may not see them again. Do not take life for granted and put your faith in a man-made ship, or in material things, but instead receive life as a blessing from God. We must understand our lives are in the hands of God, and our time on Earth is short compared to spending eternity in heaven. God has a specific plan and purpose for our lives, and desires we use what He gives us to glorify Him. Replace the icy thought of death with the warming love of Jesus Christ, who brings life everlasting.

Lord Jesus,

Thank You for saving us from death and giving us eternal life after receiving You into our hearts. Thanks for the love that can melt an iceberg and break the fear of death. I pray we would not take life for granted, and make every day count for the glory of God. I pray we would not place our trust in the things of the world, but put our lives in Your hands and trust in the plan you have for us.

"Hidden Treasure"

Genesis 9:12-17

"And God said, 'This is the token of the covenant which I make between me and you and every living creature that is with you, for perpetual generations: I do set my bow in the cloud, and it shall be for a token of a covenant between me and the earth. And it shall come to pass, when I bring a cloud over the earth, that the bow shall be seen in the cloud: And I will remember my covenant, which is between me and you and every living creature of all flesh; and the waters shall no more become a flood to destroy all flesh. And the bow shall be in the cloud; and I will look upon it, that I may remember the everlasting covenant between God and every living creature of all flesh that is upon the earth.' And God said unto Noah, 'This is the token of the covenant, which I have established between me and all flesh that is upon the earth.'"- NIV

My brother and I sat quietly at our back window, staring outside as the rain continued to fall. We patiently waited for the rain to stop so we could get back outside to play. It seemed like eternity, and just when the rain would let up, another down pour would follow within minutes. The tapping on the windowpane began to slow in pace, and eventually the rain stopped.

A beautiful rainbow stretched across the sky in brilliant colors of purple, red, green, blue, and orange. The colors were breathtaking, vibrant, and stood out like fresh paint on canvas. Immediately, I had the desire to find the gold that was buried at the end of the rainbow. I told my mom I needed to pack because I was going on an adventure to find some gold. My mother played along with me as I packed my bag of supplies and lunch for the journey. Before exiting the door, she explained to me the fable concerning rainbows and chasing pots of gold, thus cutting my adventure short.

Do you realize there is a treasure hidden in the rainbow for us, and it is no fable? The Lord made a covenant with Noah, using the rainbow as a token of a covenant between the Lord and mankind. The Lord said when a rainbow is seen in the clouds we are to remember along with Him this covenant He made with Noah. It was an expression of his love, mercy, and grace for all of mankind and every living creature on the face of the earth. The Lord loves us so much, He does not desire to be separated from us, and only wants to love us and give us the desires of our hearts. That is worth more than all the treasure you could ever find.

Every time we see a beautiful rainbow spanning across the clouds, we need to stop and thank the Lord for the treasure He has given us through his Son, Jesus Christ, and know we are part of that covenant He made a long time ago with Noah. He decided he was not going to destroy mankind again; instead, He gave us his Son, Jesus, to die and bridge the gap between God and mankind to spend eternity with Him. It is amazing to me the similarities of a rainbow and a bridge. Just think about that for a minute. So after the next rain, let's seek the treasure the Lord has for us in the simple beauty of a rainbow, and each time we set our eyes upon one, remember the Lord is reminding us just how much He loves us by giving us the greatest treasure, His one and only Son, Jesus Christ. There is no need to seek buried treasure when the treasure has been handed to us as a free gift. Accept Jesus today.

Lord Jesus,

Thank You for showing us Your love through the beauty of a rainbow. We are thankful for the meaning behind such a beautiful sight, and know You are reminding us of just how much You love and care for mankind by giving your life for us at Calvary. I pray we would take time and stop to focus more on Your beauty and creation, knowing you created it just for us, and to come to grips with the true meaning behind the treasure at the end of the rainbow.

"True Love"

John 10:11

"I am the good shepherd, The good shepherd gives his life for the sheep….No one takes it from Me, but I lay it down of Myself."- NIV

I could not wait to get to the store and pick out Valentine cards for my fifth grade class. My mind had been clouded with thoughts and feelings toward one specific girl in class. Mary was her name, and she was the first girl I had a secret crush on at school. I thought, what a great opportunity to share my feelings through a Valentine card. I was very meticulous in my selection and wanted to pick the perfect card.

Several minutes later, with the help of my mother, I selected a box that contained a series of different cards. Returning home, grabbing the bag from the backseat, I raced to my room to open the box. I poured the entire contents on my bed to find the perfect card for my secret love. Upon the selection of the card, I used one of my parent's good pens, carefully wrote "Will You Be My Valentine Mary?", sealed it inside the provided envelope, and wrote her name neatly on the front.

I was excited to get to school the next day and the only thing on my mind was the Valentine's Day party and Mary. It seemed like time stood still as I watched each minute tick away on the classroom clock. Then the moment had arrived, the teacher said, "Did everyone bring their Valentine cards and snacks?" After some simple instructions from the teacher, I reached into my brown paper bag, careful not to bend Mary's card, and distributed my cards to my fellow students. We returned back to our desks to discover a pile of Valentine cards, some snacks, and a drink.

Everyone started eating and drinking, but I was rummaging through my pile of cards, searching for Mary's card. I sat a few desks away from Mary, trying to watch her every move as she sifted through her cards. I wondered when she was going to read mine. I noticed a huge smile come across her face, and she quickly got up and began to walk towards my desk. My heart was beating like a runaway train. Then she stopped at John's desk, gave him a big hug, and said, "John, I will be your Valentine." That was my first broken heart.

There are those of us who do not have a Valentine this year, and many who suffer from broken hearts or disappointments. I do know someone who wants to be our Valentine. He loves us more than we could ever begin to imagine. He has had a crush on us from the day we were born. He continually has us on His mind, is crazy about us, and desires to love us unconditionally. He loved us so much by stretching out his arms taking nails in his perfect hands and feet dying on a wooden cross at Calvary. He watched every minute of his life drain from his body so we could spend eternity with Him forever. If that is not the greatest gift of love, then what is?

With his arms stretched wide, He is asking, "Come to Me?" He will never break our hearts, forsake us, or leave us. He desires to be our eternal Valentine, never dying, and full of abounding love. All we have to do is invite Him into our hearts, and He will do the rest. So if you are one who does not have a Valentine this year, or suffers from a broken heart, there is a fountain of life and love waiting for us to get out of our seat and walk towards Him with a smile on our face and ask, "Lord Jesus, will you be my eternal Valentine and the Lord of my life?"

Lord Jesus,

Thank You for the unconditional, never-ending love You have for us. Your love is stronger than any broken heart, disappointment, or even death. There is nothing that will ever compare to the act of Love You did for us, dying a brutal death on a cross so we could spend eternity with You in love. I pray we would love You as much as You love us, and see You as our eternal Valentine and never suffer a broken heart again.

"Wanting Nothing"

James 1:4

"But let patience have her perfect work, that ye maybe perfect and entire, wanting nothing." – KJV

Walking down the toy aisle, trying to decide what to get my friend for his birthday, my parents and I scanned over the selection of items. One toy caught my eye and screamed out my name. I had to have it, so I asked. "Mom, can I have this please?" My mother's reply was not what I wanted to hear: "Brian, we are here to shop for your friend. Maybe if you save up your allowance, you can buy it later." That was not good enough for me, so I proceeded to ask my father. "Dad, look isn't this cool, can I have it please?" Again, it was not the answer I wanted to hear.

My parents instructed me to put it back, so with my head hung in disappointment, I made my way back to where I found the toy. It was a Batman with a parachute, his arms were crossed, and he had the superhero look on his molded face. I had to have it and I had to have it now. I looked to the right and then to the left, making sure no one was looking, then I crammed it in my front pocket. Nothing else mattered, not even my parents' instructions. This feeling came over me like a breaking dam, flooding my mind with thoughts. It was like a little voice saying, "Go on, Brian, you need it, so just take it. No one is looking." Or "Just think how much fun you will have with your new Batman toy, Brian."

At six years old, I learned a very painful lesson. One, you do not disobey your parents. Two, a toy is not worth getting a red butt over, and three, I had to face the store owner and return the toy anyway. There have been a number of times in my life where I let my mind convince me that I needed something now, and did not have the patience to wait for it. Sometimes I find myself wanting it now and trying to make things happen in my own strength. To this day, I still struggle with the battle of being patient, but being a Christian and trusting in Christ has helped me to focus on wanting nothing.

The Lord knows all the desires of our hearts, so we do not even need to tell Him those desires. Faith and patience go hand-in-hand, trusting the Lord to bring what we need in His perfect timing. We need to focus on wanting nothing and keeping the Lord Jesus first in our lives, knowing He will supply all our needs so there is no reason to steal something that does not belong to us. There may be times when things seem slow moving, and waiting feels long and never-ending. The Lord will bring a desire to our heart when He feels we can handle it, and patience is the key to the perfect gift. We will not be living in disobedience, have a sore rear end, or face embarrassment for something we regret.

The enemy may try to convince us, whispering in our ear, "Come on, you need it, make it happen, you do not have time to wait." Does that sound familiar? I read a ministry newsletter that said, "When you run into some kind of trying circumstances the devil's brought your way, if you just lie down and let it run over you, it will damage you. But if you'll let patience have her perfect work, if you'll remain consistently constant, trusting in and relying confidently on the Word of God, you'll end up perfect and entire, wanting nothing." As Christians, we need to understand the Lord only desires the very best for His children, and will bring us His very best, because we are His number one priority.

Lord Jesus,

Thank You for loving us so much You died on a Cross, wanting nothing in return. Your death was a gift and all we have to do is accept it. We do not have to take it or even wait for it, as it is available to anyone who asks immediately. I pray we would take the attitude of wanting nothing and start trusting in You to bring us everything we need, according to Your will. Holy Spirit, give us patience to wait on the Lord and remember we do not need to cram anything into our pockets, as it may lead to a painful lesson.

"What Happened to Christmas?"

Colossians 1:27

"To them God has chosen to make known among the Gentiles the glorious riches of this mystery, which is Christ in you, the hope of glory." - NIV

As a young boy growing up, I remember during Christmas people would always say, "Merry Christmas." Upon meeting or just passing, it was second nature to say those two simple words. Everywhere I looked, there were those two words, big and bold, flashing, hanging, and making a statement about the true meaning of Christmas. Each year, I would look forward to hearing my dad tell us about the birth of Jesus.

What has happened to those two beautiful words? A few days ago, I was in the mall, looking for a few things, and the hardest thing for me to find were cards that said Merry Christmas. What happened to the cards portraying the celebration of the birth of our Lord and Savior? They have been replaced with Hollywood cards you can hear and record on. Every card I selected said *Happy Holiday, Seasons Greetings,* or some clever marketing slogan using characters like *The Simpsons, The Office,* or even *CSI.*

Where did Christmas go? It just does not seem the same this year. Each year, the true meaning of Christmas is slowly being forgotten. I have even caught myself a few times saying, "Have a happy holiday," instead of wishing someone a Merry Christmas. It seems like everyone is so wrapped up in the world, but if it were not for Jesus Christ, there would never have been Christmas. It can be so easy to get caught up in this new definition of Christmas, but it just is not the same.

As Christians, we must look back from the beginning and know it was prophesied that a Savior would be born to save mankind, before the word "Christmas" was ever invented by man. Jesus was not born on December 25th, a day created to originally celebrate his birth, but was quickly used for marketing and a reason to buy things we really do not need and go into debt over. What has happened to that day of celebration? It has been turned into a season of capital gain, as I heard most retail businesses make 80 percent in sales from the day after Thanksgiving to the night of Christmas Eve.

What has happened to Jesus? I have even noticed churches tailoring their Christmas specials, some even taking Jesus completely out of the picture. What kind of impression are we sending to the next generation? As Christians, we must remember Jesus Christ lives in us and through us. If it were not for His birth, we would not have our salvation, better than any Christmas gift we will ever find under the tree. Jesus Christ is the hope and glory that lives within us, and we should be celebrating Him every day.

Everything said in the Bible about His birth to the present has come to pass, and that gives me hope of His quick return. I am just as guilty as others, as I can easily get caught up in this commercialized Christmas and forget the beautiful story buried in the marketing plan designed by man. We need to be a torch in the darkness and burn bright for Jesus Christ daily, and be different because we are not of this world. Christians are called to be different and to reflect the character of Jesus to those around us.

Let me challenge you to be different and allow Christ in you to minister to people about the true meaning behind the words "Merry Christmas." You could take away all the presents, trees, decorations, and one thing will never change. The fact Jesus was born to save mankind from their sins. That is the only thing that matters. Jesus Christ wants the greatest gift, and that is for all of mankind to call upon His name for Salvation. He was born for that reason, not just for Christmas.

Lord Jesus,

Thank You for coming to the earth in human form, being born in a dirty manger and ministering Your love to mankind through your sacrifice on the cross. You are the true meaning of Christmas, as each year the world tries to shut You out more. I pray we would celebrate Christmas every day, because you have given us the greatest gift our salvation, and Your daily gift of grace, mercy, and love sustains us.

I pray all would wake up each morning and unwrap their present of You in their lives.

"Ride of a Lifetime"

Psalm 27:1

"The Lord is my light and my salvation; whom shall I fear? The Lord is my strength of my life; of whom shall I be afraid?" – KJV

Proverbs 8:35

"For whoso findeth me findeth life, and shall obtain favor of the Lord." - KJV

Waist bar pulled to my lap, shoulder bar snug in place, I felt like a sardine in a can. The wheels were set in motion and the car made its way up a steep incline that seemed to take hours, but within minutes we were at the top of the track. The car slowly crept to the starting point, allowing me to look straight down to the tiny onlookers below. I was 250 feet up in the air, and strapped into a tin can. The car hung in suspension for five seconds before dropping almost straight down.

My breath was taken away from the fall combined with a yell deep down in my stomach. I looked over and saw my brother and aunt were suffering from the same effects. This roller coaster was so fast and powerful, I had little time to catch my breath and find my sense of direction. It truly was a ride of a lifetime, and such a rush to ride. Matter of fact, my brother and I rode it again just to catch the rush again.

The roller coaster was called SheiKra, located at Bush Gardens in Orlando, FL. Our Aunt Linda told us the night before that we had to ride with her. She explained the incredible climb, descending drop, and the three loops with all the twists and turns. Talking about it was one thing, but riding it was a whole new adventure. We were the only three in our party brave enough to ride this monster.

Have you even been on one of those rides that take your breath away and give you a ride you will never forget? As Christians, we can find that feeling in walking with the Lord on a daily basis. He will take our breath away, as we are in awe of how he moves like a roller coaster in our lives. He will be with us at the highest point, deep in the valley, and through every loop, twist, and turn in life.

We can talk about a personal relationship with Jesus Christ, but talking about it and doing it are like night and day. The Lord desires we all take the ride of a lifetime and feel the daily rush of life with the Lord. The fastest roller coaster in the world could never compare to the ride we can have with Jesus. All we have to do is call to Jesus and ask Him to take control of our lives, and then hang on for the adventure.

Lord Jesus,

Thank You for sacrificing your life on the cross to give us abundant, eternal life with You. You desire all to join You for the ride of a lifetime. I pray we trust You in the peaks, valleys, loops, and turns in life, knowing You will bring us safely through to the end. I pray those who do not know you personally would call on your name, step into life with You, pull down their lap bar, and prepare for the ride of their lives.